Restorative Reentry

Restorative Reentry

By Brandon O'Brien

Table of contents

Introduction

When it comes to the reentry process for individuals released from prison, there's a shocking fact that can't be ignored. According to recent studies, a staggering 67% of released prisoners are rearrested within three years. This statistic is not only alarming but also highlights the struggles faced by those trying to reintegrate into society after incarceration. It's a problem that I, Brandon O'Brien, intimately understand, as I too have experienced the challenges of reentry firsthand.

My personal journey with incarceration has transformed my life and ignited a passion within me to help others navigate the complex path of reentry. I know what it's like to face the judgment and stigma that follows you after release. But I've also discovered the power of restorative practices in healing, rebuilding relationships, and creating a better future. That's why I've dedicated myself to sharing these practices with others, in the hope of inspiring change and creating a more supportive environment for individuals in the reentry process.

The need for restorative reentry is more pressing than ever. Traditional methods have proven inadequate in addressing the root causes of crime and reintegrating individuals into society. It's time for a paradigm shift towards a restorative model that focuses on healing, building relationships, and repairing the harm caused by crime or incarceration. This approach not only benefits individuals in their journey towards reentry but also promotes a safer and more compassionate society as a whole.

But what exactly do we mean by restorative practices? At its core, restorative practices involve a set of principles and values that guide the way we approach reentry. It's about recognizing the humanity of individuals who have been incarcerated and providing opportunities for healing, growth, and reconciliation. By fostering self-reflection and personal accountability, restorative practices enable individuals to confront and address their past actions, emotions, and trauma, ultimately leading to transformative change.

One of the greatest challenges faced by individuals during reentry is reconnecting with their families. The strain caused by incarceration can lead to broken trust and strained relationships. However, restorative practices offer a path towards rebuilding and repairing these connections. By creating a supportive environment that encourages open dialogue, empathy, and understanding, we can heal the wounds caused by separation and work towards building stronger and healthier relationships.

But restorative reentry goes beyond the individual and extends into the community. It's the community's role to offer support, understanding, and opportunities for growth to those reintegrating into society. Restorative practices can foster empathy, collaboration, and a shared responsibility for successful reentry. By building bridges between individuals who have been incarcerated and community members, we can create a network of support that paves the way for a brighter future.

Of course, systemic barriers still persist and pose significant challenges to successful reentry. Discrimination, limited opportunities, and societal stigmas all hinder the process of healing and reintegration. That's where restorative practices play a crucial role. By addressing these systemic barriers head-on and advocating for changes in policies, laws, and social norms, we can create a more just and inclusive society that values the potential for growth and transformation.

At the heart of restorative reentry lies the concept of transformative justice. Unlike traditional punitive approaches, transformative justice seeks to address the root causes of harm and promote healing rather than punishment and retribution. It's about creating opportunities for growth, fostering empathy, and working towards a society where everyone has the chance to thrive. Restorative practices are the vehicle through which transformative justice can be achieved.

As we embark on this journey towards restorative reentry, I invite you to join me. In the pages that follow, we will explore practical strategies and tools for implementing restorative practices in your own life and community. Together, we can make a difference, one story of transformation at a time. So, let's dive in and discover the potential benefits that restorative reentry holds for all of us.

Chapter 1: The Significance of Restorative Reentry in Supporting Individuals Post Incarceration

Why Restorative Reentry Matters

Restorative reentry is a concept that holds immense significance in ensuring successful reintegration into society. Unlike traditional punitive approaches, restorative practices emphasize healing, reconciliation, and personal growth. In order to understand the importance of restorative reentry, it is essential to explore its historical context, cultural influences, and religious perspectives.

The historical development of restorative practices provides insight into their evolution and implementation. Throughout history, various restorative justice principles have been applied, demonstrating the enduring relevance of this approach. By examining these historical examples, we can better understand the efficacy of restorative reentry in addressing the needs of individuals transitioning back into society.

Furthermore, the cultural context surrounding restorative practices plays a crucial role in determining their effectiveness. Different cultures and societies have embraced or rejected these practices based on their own values and belief systems. By analyzing these cultural factors, we can gain a deeper understanding of how restorative reentry can be tailored to specific contexts, ensuring its success.

Religious teachings and beliefs have long been proponents of restorative justice, emphasizing the importance of forgiveness, reconciliation, and rehabilitation. Religious communities have incorporated restorative practices into their reentry programs, recognizing their transformative potential. By examining the religious perspectives on restorative reentry, we can gain insight into the spiritual principles that guide this approach.

Religious rituals and ceremonies also play a significant role in facilitating healing and reconciliation during the reentry process. These rituals offer individuals the opportunity to rebuild their lives and relationships, providing a path towards redemption and restoration. Understanding the impact of these rituals on the reentry journey is vital for developing effective restorative reentry programs.

Religious leaders have played a pivotal role in advocating for restorative practices within the criminal justice system. Their influence and efforts have brought attention to the transformative potential of restorative reentry and have prompted religious organizations to support successful reintegration. Exploring the role of religious leaders in this advocacy can shed light on the power of collective action in creating lasting change.

Religious communities, as support networks, have a unique role to play in assisting individuals during the reintegration process. They provide essential support and resources, helping individuals navigate the challenges they may face. By analyzing the impact of religious communities on successful reentry, we can develop a comprehensive understanding of the vital role they play in facilitating positive outcomes.

Spirituality is also closely intertwined with the process of restorative reentry. The role of spirituality in personal growth and transformation cannot be underestimated. Spiritual practices and beliefs contribute to individuals' ability to heal, grow, and reintegrate into society. By exploring the role of spirituality in restorative reentry, we can gain insight into the holistic nature of this approach.

Religious institutions have implemented specific restorative reentry programs, offering a structured and supportive environment for individuals transitioning back into society. By examining the effectiveness and impact of these programs, we can assess their contribution to successful reintegration and identify best practices for future implementation.

Finally, it is essential to consider the intersection between religious and secular approaches to restorative reentry. By comparing and contrasting these approaches, we can identify areas where they complement each other and work towards a common goal of successful reintegration. Understanding this intersection allows for the development of comprehensive and inclusive strategies that maximize the potential for positive outcomes.

In conclusion, restorative reentry matters for a multitude of reasons. By exploring the concept from a religious perspective, we gain valuable insights into the principles, practices, and support networks that contribute to successful reintegration. This exploration provides a foundation for understanding the transformative potential of restorative reentry and the importance of incorporating it into the criminal justice system.

About the Author

Introduction to the subchapter "About the Author."

When it comes to restorative reentry, understanding the author's background is crucial for establishing credibility and context. In this section, I will provide an introduction to myself, Brandon O'Brien, and share my personal journey and expertise on restorative reentry.

Briefly, my journey has been shaped by personal experiences and a deep commitment to helping individuals successfully reintegrate into society. These experiences have given me unique insights and approaches that I am excited to share with you.

My personal journey and experiences related to restorative reentry have played a significant role in shaping my understanding of this field. As someone who has personally experienced the challenges of reentry, I bring a firsthand perspective that can resonate with individuals going through the same process. These experiences have given me empathy and a deep understanding of the struggles and obstacles individuals face during their reentry journey.

In terms of qualifications, I have dedicated years to researching and studying restorative reentry. This includes professional qualifications and training in the field, which have equipped me with the necessary tools to guide others through the reentry process. My expertise is not just theoretical, but grounded in practical knowledge and real-world applications.

Furthermore, my involvement in the restorative reentry community has allowed me to contribute to the field in meaningful ways. I have been actively involved in various organizations and initiatives that promote restorative practices and support individuals during their reentry journey. Through these involvements, I have had the privilege of witnessing firsthand the transformative impact that restorative reentry can have on individuals and communities.

What sets me apart is my unique perspective on restorative reentry. I bring fresh insights and innovative ideas to the table, challenging traditional approaches and offering new strategies to address the challenges of reentry. Through my work, I have developed practical tools and techniques that have helped countless individuals overcome barriers and achieve positive outcomes.

My expertise and personal journey make me a credible and trustworthy source for anyone navigating the reentry process. I firmly believe that having an author with firsthand experience and knowledge in the subject matter is essential in providing practical guidance and support. Many individuals have benefited from my insights and guidance, and their testimonials attest to the impact I have had on their lives.

The impact I have made in the restorative reentry field is a testament to the power of this approach. I have witnessed numerous success stories and positive outcomes resulting from my work. These stories are not just about individuals achieving personal growth, but also about the wider impact on their families and communities. Restorative reentry has the potential to create a ripple effect of positive change that extends far beyond the individual.

Now, you may be wondering, how does my personal journey and expertise relate to you, the reader? My insights and guidance can benefit anyone going through the reentry process or those involved in supporting reentry efforts. By implementing restorative reentry practices, individuals can find a path to positive change and growth, ultimately leading to successful reintegration into society.

In summary, understanding the author, Brandon O'Brien, and his personal journey and expertise on restorative reentry is paramount. Through my personal experiences, professional qualifications, involvement in the restorative reentry community, and unique perspective, I bring valuable insights and guidance to help individuals navigate the challenges of reentry and promote successful reintegration into society.

Target Audience

As I sit down to write this book, I am acutely aware of the specific audience I am addressing - individuals who are in the process of releasing from prison and their allies. It is crucial to understand this audience in order to effectively address their needs and challenges. The journey of reentry is not an easy one, and it is important to recognize the unique challenges that these individuals face upon their release.

Finding employment, stable housing, and reconnecting with family and friends are just a few of the hurdles that people releasing from prison often encounter. The social stigmas and barriers they face can be overwhelming, making it even more difficult to navigate their way back into society. It is essential for allies, such as family members, friends, and community organizations, to step in and play a crucial role in supporting these individuals during this transition. Allies can provide practical and emotional support, offering a helping hand when it is needed most.

One aspect that often goes unnoticed is the psychological impact of incarceration. Trauma, anxiety, and difficulty adjusting to life outside of prison are all common experiences for those who have been incarcerated. It is imperative to recognize and address these psychological challenges in order to support successful reintegration. Each individual within the target audience has unique needs and experiences, and it is vital to provide tailored support and resources that meet these challenges. Factors such as gender, race, and length of incarceration must be taken into account to ensure effective assistance.

In addition to individual challenges, there are also systemic barriers that individuals releasing from prison may face. Limited access to education and employment opportunities are just a few examples of these barriers. It is essential for policies and programs to be in place that address these issues and promote successful reintegration.

Building a supportive community is of utmost significance in the reentry process. Peer support, mentorship, and networks of individuals who have successfully reintegrated into society can all contribute to a supportive environment. By fostering a sense of belonging and community, we can provide the necessary foundation for these individuals to thrive.

While support from allies and community is crucial, it is equally important to empower individuals releasing from prison to take ownership of their own reintegration process. Self-reflection, goal-setting, and personal growth are all integral components of this journey. By empowering individuals to take control of their own lives, we can foster a sense of agency and responsibility.

Collaboration and partnerships between government agencies, community organizations, and stakeholders are vital in providing comprehensive support to the target audience. By pooling resources and expertise, we can address the various needs and challenges that individuals face during reentry.

Even with all the progress we have made, there is still a pressing need for continued advocacy and support for individuals releasing from prison and their allies. It is crucial that we continue to improve reintegration programs, policies, and social attitudes towards this population. Together, we can create a society that embraces and supports the successful reentry of these individuals, allowing them to lead fulfilling and productive lives.

Book Format

As a writer, I have come to appreciate the importance of book format in providing structure and organization for readers. The way a book is formatted can make a significant difference in guiding readers through the content and ensuring that they can easily navigate through the information. In this book, Restorative Reentry, I aim to create a format that is not only informative but also engaging and easy to follow.

Chapters play a crucial role in the structure of a book. They divide the content into manageable sections, allowing readers to digest the information in a more structured manner. Furthermore, chapters help readers navigate through the book by providing clear breaks and transitions between different topics or themes. Without chapters, a book can easily become overwhelming and difficult to follow.

One often overlooked aspect of chapters is their titles. Chapter titles serve as a preview of the content within, giving readers an idea of what to expect. Intriguing and well-crafted chapter titles can pique readers' curiosity and draw them further into the book. In Restorative Reentry, I have taken great care in crafting chapter titles that are both informative and attention-grabbing, ensuring that readers are compelled to delve deeper into the content.

The structure of chapters is also worth mentioning. Typically, a chapter consists of an introduction, body, and conclusion. This structure provides a clear framework for presenting information and allows readers to follow along easily. However, it's important to note that the length and format of chapters can vary depending on the genre and the author's style. Some chapters may be short and concise, while others may be more extensive and detailed. It all depends on the specific needs of the book and its target audience.

Subchapters, on the other hand, provide further organization and structure within chapters. They break down the content into smaller sections, making it easier for readers to navigate and comprehend. In Restorative Reentry, I have included subchapters to divide chapters into subtopics and provide additional information within specific themes. This not only enhances the reading experience but also allows readers to easily locate and revisit specific sections of interest.

Numerous books effectively utilize subchapters to enhance the reading experience. They serve as signposts, guiding readers through the content and ensuring that they can easily find the information they seek. Examples of such books include "The 4-Hour Workweek" by Tim Ferriss, "Atomic Habits" by James Clear, and "Deep Work" by Cal Newport. These books demonstrate how subchapters can add depth and clarity to the overall structure of a book.

The benefits of using subchapters are numerous. They improve readability and comprehension by breaking down complex information into smaller, digestible chunks. Furthermore, subchapters allow readers to easily navigate to specific sections of interest, saving them time and effort. In Restorative Reentry, I have carefully considered the benefits of using subchapters and have strategically incorporated them to enhance the flow and structure of the book.

However, it's essential to maintain a balance when using subchapters. Too many subchapters can make a book feel fragmented and disjointed, while too few can make it difficult for readers to navigate through the content. Therefore, subchapters should be used strategically, ensuring that they enhance the overall flow and structure of the book without overwhelming the reader.

Formatting is another crucial aspect of chapters and subchapters. By visually distinguishing them through formatting choices such as different fonts, headings, or numbering, readers can easily identify and differentiate between chapters and subchapters. This not only improves the overall reading experience but also adds a visual element to the book, making it more engaging and aesthetically pleasing.

In conclusion, the format of a book, including chapters and subchapters, plays a vital role in providing structure and organization. By carefully considering the needs and preferences of the readers, authors can create a format that enhances the overall reading experience. Restorative Reentry aims to deliver information in a clear and engaging manner, utilizing chapters and subchapters to guide readers through the content effectively. I believe that the structure and format of a book can greatly enhance the reader's experience, and I hope that this book achieves just that.

Book Language

As I delve into the topic of book language in my book Restorative Reentry, I am reminded of the importance of clarifying the language in which a book is written. This seemingly small detail can have a significant impact on a reader's experience and understanding of the book. Without clear language clarification, confusion and misunderstandings can easily arise, leading to frustration and disappointment.

To illustrate this point, let me present a hypothetical scenario. Imagine a reader excitedly purchasing a book without knowing the language in which it is written. As they eagerly begin reading, they soon realize that they cannot understand a single word. The anticipation quickly turns into frustration and disappointment as they find themselves unable to engage with the book's content. This scenario highlights the potential consequences of not clarifying the language of a book before purchasing it.

In this hypothetical situation, there are a few assumptions and conditions to consider. The reader did not have access to information about the book's language before purchasing it. They assumed that the book would be in their native language or a language they are familiar with. These assumptions, while understandable, highlight the need for authors and publishers to provide clear language clarification to avoid such disappointment.

Clarifying the language of a book is of utmost importance. It allows readers to make informed decisions about purchasing or reading a book. By knowing the language, readers can align their expectations and ensure that the content is accessible to them. Additionally, clarifying the language can prevent misunderstandings and dissatisfaction, saving both readers and authors from wasted time and effort.

There are various ways to clarify the language of a book. Bookstores and online retailers often provide language information in book descriptions, helping readers make informed choices. Additionally, publishers can include a language label on book covers or spines, making it easily identifiable. These simple methods can go a long way in ensuring that readers have the necessary language information before purchasing a book.

The impact of clarifying a book's language on its sales should not be underestimated. Clear language information can attract readers who are specifically looking for books in a particular language. On the other hand, ambiguous or missing language information may deter potential readers, resulting in lost sales. Publishers and authors must recognize the importance of language clarification in maximizing the reach and impact of their work.

However, it is not solely the responsibility of publishers and authors to ensure that readers have the necessary language information. Readers also have a responsibility in actively seeking out language details before making a purchase. Relying solely on assumptions or expectations can lead to disappointment. By being proactive and diligent in gathering language information, readers can avoid unnecessary frustration.

Publishers, too, have a responsibility in providing clear language information. Accurate and easily accessible language details should be included in book marketing materials. Transparency should be prioritized, and misleading or ambiguous language information should be avoided. By taking these steps, publishers can foster trust with their readers and ensure a positive reading experience.

It is important to acknowledge the potential language barriers that readers may face when purchasing or reading books. Translating books into different languages and ensuring linguistic accuracy is a challenging task. The publishing industry should strive for language diversity and inclusivity, allowing readers from various linguistic backgrounds to access a wide range of content.

In conclusion, the language in which a book is written is a crucial factor in readers' satisfaction and informed decision-making. Clarifying the language not only prevents misunderstandings and disappointment but also maximizes the book's reach and impact. It is the joint responsibility of readers, publishers, and authors to ensure that language details are clearly communicated. In the next subchapter, I will explore another essential aspect of restorative reentry.

Chapter 2: Understanding Restorative Justice

Restorative Justice Defined

Introduction to Restorative Justice:

Restorative justice is a transformative approach to the criminal justice system that focuses on repairing harm, promoting accountability, and fostering community involvement. Unlike traditional punitive justice, which prioritizes punishment and isolation, restorative justice seeks to address the needs of victims, empower offenders to take responsibility for their actions, and facilitate healing within the community. By shifting the focus from punishment to restoration, restorative justice offers a fresh perspective on how we can address the complexities of crime and provide meaningful pathways for individuals to reintegrate into society.

Historical and Philosophical Origins:

To truly understand the principles and philosophy behind restorative justice, it is essential to explore its historical and philosophical origins. Restorative justice traces its roots back to indigenous cultures, where community healing and reconciliation were integral components of justice systems. Movements such as the Victim-Offender Reconciliation Program and the Truth and Reconciliation Commission in South Africa played crucial roles in shaping the modern concept of restorative justice.

At its core, restorative justice is guided by the belief that crime is not just a violation of laws, but a rupture of relationships and a disruption of the community's well-being. Drawing on principles of empathy, compassion, and dialogue, restorative justice seeks to repair the harm caused by crime and restore relationships between victims, offenders, and the wider community.

Key Principles of Restorative Justice:

The key principles of restorative justice form the foundation upon which the entire process is built. Accountability is a central principle, emphasizing that offenders must take responsibility for their actions and actively work towards repairing the harm they have caused. Repairing harm involves addressing the needs of the victim and the wider community, seeking to heal the wounds inflicted by the crime. Community involvement is vital in the restorative justice process, as it recognizes the importance of collective responsibility and the role of the community in supporting the healing and reintegration of both victims and offenders.

Victim-Centered Approach:

Restorative justice places a significant emphasis on meeting the needs and experiences of victims. By actively involving victims in the process, restorative justice aims to empower them and provide a space for their voices to be heard. Through facilitated dialogue and empathy-building, restorative justice creates an environment where victims can share their stories, express their emotions, and have a say in the outcome. This focus on the victim's perspective not only promotes healing but also contributes to the prevention of future harm by addressing the underlying causes of crime.

Offender Accountability and Rehabilitation:

In traditional punitive justice systems, the focus often lies solely on punishment, neglecting the potential for offender rehabilitation and reintegration. Restorative justice takes a different approach, recognizing that offenders can change and offering them opportunities for personal growth and transformation. By holding offenders accountable for their actions and providing support for rehabilitation, restorative justice seeks to break the cycle of crime and reduce recidivism rates. This approach acknowledges the inherent dignity of every individual and provides a pathway for their successful reentry into society.

Community Involvement and Support:

Restorative justice recognizes that the community plays a vital role in the healing and restoration process. Community members are actively involved in the restorative justice process, whether it be through participating in victim-offender mediations, serving as mentors for offenders, or offering support to victims. By engaging the community, restorative justice not only promotes a sense of collective responsibility but also fosters a greater understanding of the complex issues surrounding crime and the importance of prevention.

Restorative Practices and Techniques:

Various restorative practices and techniques are employed within the restorative justice framework to facilitate communication, understanding, and resolution. Victim-offender mediation and conferencing are examples of these practices, where facilitated dialogues allow victims and offenders to come together to discuss the impact of the crime, address concerns, and work towards a mutually agreed-upon resolution. These practices encourage active participation and empower individuals to take ownership of their actions, facilitating the restoration of relationships and promoting a sense of justice.

Cultural Considerations in Restorative Justice:

Restorative justice is not a one-size-fits-all approach, as it is influenced by cultural values and norms. Different cultures may have unique approaches and interpretations of restorative justice, reflecting the diversity and richness of our global community. Recognizing and respecting these cultural variations is essential in creating inclusive and effective restorative justice practices. Cultural sensitivity and inclusivity are vital in ensuring that restorative justice is accessible and applicable to all individuals, regardless of their background or heritage.

Critiques and Challenges:

Despite its numerous benefits, restorative justice is not without its critiques and challenges. Some argue that it may prioritize the needs of offenders over those of victims, potentially retraumatizing victims in the process. The implementation of restorative justice on a broader scale also presents logistical and resource challenges, requiring significant investment in training, infrastructure, and community support. Addressing these critiques and challenges requires ongoing dialogue and collaboration, finding ways to strike a balance between the needs of all stakeholders involved.

Impact and Future of Restorative Justice:

Restorative justice has made significant strides in various contexts, ranging from schools to criminal justice systems. Its impact is evident in the transformational experiences of individuals who have participated in restorative justice processes. Looking ahead, the future of restorative justice holds great promise. As our understanding of its principles deepens, and as more communities and justice systems embrace its potential, restorative justice has the power to fundamentally transform the criminal justice system. By prioritizing healing, accountability, and community involvement, restorative justice offers a beacon of hope for a more just and compassionate society.

Benefits of Restorative Justice

Introduction to Restorative Justice

Restorative justice is a transformative approach to addressing crime and conflict, centered around repairing harm and restoring relationships. It is a departure from the traditional punitive model, focusing on accountability, healing, and personal growth for both offenders and victims. In the context of reentry, restorative justice offers a promising alternative to the prevailing retributive system.

Restorative justice in reentry involves bringing together individuals impacted by crime, including offenders, victims, and community members, to collectively address the harm caused and find ways to repair it. Through facilitated dialogues and processes, participants are given the opportunity to share their perspectives, express their feelings, and collaboratively develop solutions that promote healing and reintegration.

The positive outcomes and advantages of restorative practices are manifold. By prioritizing dialogue and understanding, restorative justice has been shown to reduce recidivism rates significantly. Offenders who engage in restorative processes are more likely to take responsibility for their actions, understand the impact of their behavior on others, and actively work towards making amends.

Moreover, restorative practices have the power to foster personal growth and accountability among offenders. By engaging in meaningful conversations with victims, offenders gain insights into the consequences of their actions and are motivated to make positive changes in their lives. This increased sense of accountability promotes rehabilitation and reintegration, ultimately leading to a reduction in future criminal behavior.

In addition to personal growth, restorative justice also holds the potential for improved mental health outcomes for offenders. Traditional punishment often exacerbates feelings of shame, guilt, and isolation, which can contribute to mental health issues. In contrast, restorative practices offer a supportive environment where offenders can address their emotions, repair relationships, and work towards holistic healing.

The Impact of Restorative Justice on Victims

One of the significant advantages of restorative justice is its potential to provide victims with a sense of closure and healing. By engaging in face-to-face dialogues with their offenders, victims are given the opportunity to express their pain, ask questions, and receive answers. This process can bring a profound sense of validation and validation, allowing victims to find closure and move forward in their healing journey.

Restorative practices also empower victims by giving them an active role in the justice process. Instead of being passive bystanders, victims become active participants, shaping the outcomes and decisions related to their case. This empowerment can help restore agency and control, enabling victims to reclaim their lives and regain a sense of justice.

Moreover, restorative justice facilitates the restoration of relationships between victims and offenders. By creating a safe space for open and honest communication, restorative processes enable both parties to address the harm caused and explore possibilities for reconciliation. This can be particularly valuable for victims who seek a sense of understanding, forgiveness, or even the potential for rebuilding trust.

The Impact of Restorative Justice on Communities

Restorative justice has far-reaching benefits for communities as well. By focusing on repairing harm and addressing the underlying causes of crime, restorative practices contribute to community safety and cohesion. Rather than perpetuating cycles of violence and retribution, restorative justice seeks to break these cycles by promoting understanding, empathy, and healing.

Restorative practices also offer a unique opportunity to address the root causes of crime. By engaging in conversations that explore the underlying factors that contribute to criminal behavior, such as poverty, trauma, or lack of social support, restorative justice aims to identify and address these systemic issues. This holistic approach not only reduces individual harm but also works towards creating a safer and more just society.

Additionally, restorative justice builds trust and social capital within communities. By involving community members in the restorative processes, a sense of collective responsibility and accountability is fostered. This collaborative approach creates stronger social bonds, enhances community resilience, and encourages individuals to actively participate in creating safer neighborhoods.

The Cultural Perspective on Restorative Justice

To truly understand the impact and effectiveness of restorative justice, it is essential to consider the cultural perspectives and themes that shape its implementation. Different cultures view and approach restorative practices in distinct ways, influenced by their values, traditions, and historical contexts.

For instance, in indigenous cultures, restorative justice aligns closely with their traditional dispute resolution practices. These communities often prioritize collective healing, community involvement, and interconnectedness. In contrast, Western societies may emphasize individual accountability and personal growth.

Understanding these cultural factors is crucial because they can significantly influence the effectiveness of restorative justice in reentry. Cultural competence becomes paramount in implementing restorative practices that resonate with the values and beliefs of the individuals and communities involved. By acknowledging and respecting diverse cultural perspectives, restorative justice can be tailored to be more inclusive and impactful.

Cross-Cultural Case Studies

Examining cross-cultural case studies provides valuable insights into the diverse ways restorative justice is applied and its outcomes in different cultural contexts. By exploring examples from various countries or communities, we can identify commonalities and differences, shedding light on what works and what can be improved.

For instance, in New Zealand's Māori community, restorative justice practices, known as "peacemaking circles," have been widely implemented. These circles bring together offenders, victims, and community members in a safe and respectful space, emphasizing dialogue, understanding, and healing. The outcomes have been promising, with reduced recidivism rates and strengthened community connections.

Similarly, in Uganda, restorative justice programs have focused on post-conflict reconciliation, particularly in the aftermath of the civil war. By engaging both victims and perpetrators in truth-telling dialogues and community-based ceremonies, these programs have contributed to healing, forgiveness, and community reintegration.

These cross-cultural case studies highlight the significance of cultural adaptation and understanding in restorative justice. By learning from different approaches, we can gain valuable insights into how restorative practices can be effectively tailored to specific cultural contexts, enhancing their impact and relevance.

The Role of Cultural Competence in Restorative Justice

Cultural competence plays a pivotal role in the successful implementation of restorative justice. Practitioners and stakeholders must possess a deep understanding of diverse cultures, traditions, and perspectives to ensure that restorative processes are inclusive, respectful, and effective.

By developing cultural competence, practitioners can better navigate the complexities of diverse cultural contexts, communicate effectively, and build trust with individuals and communities. Cultural competence allows for the recognition and incorporation of cultural values, norms, and practices into restorative processes, making them more meaningful and impactful.

Strategies for developing cultural competence can include ongoing education and training, engagement with diverse communities, and the establishment of partnerships with cultural organizations. By actively seeking to expand their cultural knowledge and understanding, practitioners can enhance their ability to facilitate restorative processes that honor the unique needs and perspectives of all involved.

Challenges and Future Directions

While restorative justice holds immense promise, it is not without its challenges and limitations, particularly in a cross-cultural context. Cultural differences can present barriers to effective communication, understanding, and implementation of restorative practices.

Language barriers, differing worldviews, and power dynamics within communities can all impact the success of restorative justice initiatives. Recognizing and addressing these challenges is crucial for fostering inclusivity and ensuring that the potential benefits of restorative justice are realized by all.

Potential solutions and strategies for overcoming these challenges lie in embracing cultural humility, actively seeking input from diverse voices, and engaging in ongoing dialogue and learning. By continuously adapting and evolving restorative practices to address cultural nuances, we can promote greater equity, understanding, and effectiveness.

Looking towards the future, research and practice in restorative justice must continue to evolve. Further studies exploring the intersection of cultural factors and restorative practices can deepen our understanding of how different cultural contexts impact outcomes. Additionally, efforts should be made to develop standardized frameworks that integrate cultural competence into the implementation of restorative justice.

In conclusion, restorative justice offers a transformative approach to reentry, promoting healing, accountability, and community safety. By recognizing and addressing the impact of restorative practices on offenders, victims, and communities, we can build a more just and inclusive society. Cultural competence is integral to this process, ensuring that restorative justice is implemented in a way that respects and honors diverse cultural perspectives. Challenges and limitations exist, but through ongoing dialogue, research, and learning, the potential for restorative justice to create lasting positive change is immense.

Applying Restorative Justice in Reentry

Introduction:

Restorative justice is a concept that has gained recognition for its transformative approach to crime and punishment. In this subchapter, we will delve into how restorative justice can be applied to support individuals releasing from prison. The reentry process can be overwhelming and challenging, and providing the necessary support is crucial to ensure successful reintegration. By incorporating restorative justice principles, we can create a more compassionate and effective system that promotes healing, accountability, and community involvement.

Anecdote:

Let me share with you the story of John, a man who has experienced firsthand the difficulties of reentering society after serving time in prison. John faced numerous challenges during his reentry process, from finding stable housing and employment to navigating strained relationships with family and friends. If restorative justice principles had been applied in his case, John could have received the support and guidance needed to address these challenges in a holistic and compassionate manner. Instead, he felt isolated and lost, with little hope for a better future.

Understanding Restorative Justice:

Restorative justice is a paradigm that focuses on repairing harm caused by crime through the active participation of all parties involved. Its key principles include taking responsibility, promoting healing and reintegration, and involving the community. Rather than emphasizing punishment and retribution, restorative justice aims to address the underlying causes of crime and create opportunities for personal growth and transformation. By recognizing the importance of repairing harm and fostering understanding, we can create a more just and equitable society.

Restorative Approaches in Reentry Programs:

When it comes to supporting individuals releasing from prison, restorative justice principles can be invaluable. Reentry programs that incorporate these principles recognize the importance of involving both the person who has been released and the community. By fostering dialogue and promoting understanding, these programs provide a platform for healing and reconciliation. For example, victim-offender dialogues or community conferences allow individuals to address the harm caused by their actions and work towards making amends. By including all parties affected by the crime, these restorative approaches help rebuild trust and restore relationships.

Addressing the Needs of Individuals Releasing from Prison:

The needs of individuals reentering society after being incarcerated are multifaceted and complex. Restorative justice can play a crucial role in addressing these needs by providing support, resources, and opportunities for personal growth. Many individuals leaving prison face challenges such as finding employment, accessing housing, and rebuilding relationships. By adopting a restorative approach, we can ensure that these individuals have access to the necessary support systems and resources to successfully reintegrate into society. Through mentorship programs and community support, we can help them navigate the obstacles they encounter and foster a sense of belonging and purpose.

Building Supportive Relationships:

One of the key factors in successful reentry is the presence of supportive relationships. Restorative justice practices, such as circle processes or mentoring programs, can be instrumental in helping individuals connect with their communities and build positive relationships. By providing a space for dialogue and understanding, these practices facilitate the creation of a supportive network that can provide guidance, accountability, and emotional support. Through these relationships, individuals can find the strength and encouragement needed to overcome challenges and stay on a positive path.

Promoting Accountability and Responsibility:

Restorative justice places a strong emphasis on promoting accountability and responsibility among individuals releasing from prison. Rather than solely focusing on punishment, this approach encourages individuals to recognize the harm they caused and take steps to repair it. By facilitating the process of making amends, restorative justice provides an opportunity for personal growth and transformation. By holding individuals accountable for their actions in a constructive and compassionate manner, we can help them develop a sense of ownership and responsibility, which is crucial for successful reintegration.

Addressing Trauma and Healing:

It is essential to acknowledge that many individuals who have been incarcerated have experienced trauma. Restorative justice offers a healing-centered approach to addressing this trauma, recognizing the importance of trauma-informed care and support. By creating an environment that is sensitive to the experiences of those who have been traumatized, we can help individuals heal and break the cycle of violence. Through counseling, therapy, and other supportive interventions, restorative justice can provide the tools necessary for individuals to address and overcome the trauma they have experienced.

Community Involvement and Reintegration:

The role of the community in supporting individuals releasing from prison cannot be overstated. Restorative justice principles emphasize the importance of community involvement and active participation in the reentry process. By fostering a sense of belonging and acceptance, the community can play a vital role in promoting successful reintegration. Through volunteer programs, employment opportunities, and support networks, the community can provide individuals with the necessary resources and opportunities to rebuild their lives. In turn, this involvement benefits the community as a whole, creating safer and more inclusive neighborhoods.

Conclusion and Final Thoughts:

In conclusion, applying restorative justice principles to support individuals releasing from prison is crucial for their successful reintegration into society. By repairing harm, promoting healing, and involving all parties affected by the crime, we can create a more compassionate and effective system. It is imperative that we recognize the importance of support, resources, and opportunities for personal growth in addressing the needs of those reentering society. Through building supportive relationships, promoting accountability, addressing trauma, and involving the community, we can create a reentry process that is transformative and promotes a sense of belonging and purpose. Let us strive towards a society that values restoration and healing, offering a second chance to those who have paid their debt to society.

Case Studies

Introduction to Case Studies

Understanding successful restorative reentry programs is crucial in order to pave the way for effective rehabilitation and successful reintegration of individuals into society. Case studies provide invaluable insights into real-life examples of these programs, allowing us to examine their impact and identify key factors that contribute to their success.

In this subchapter, we will explore various case studies that shed light on the transformative power of restorative reentry programs. By delving into the stories of these programs, we can gain a deeper understanding of their origins, objectives, components, and outcomes. Each case study presents a unique approach to restorative reentry, highlighting the diverse strategies and interventions employed to support individuals in their journey towards a brighter future.

Case Study 1: The First Chance Program

The First Chance Program, born out of a commitment to provide individuals with a fresh start, has proven to be a game-changer in reducing recidivism rates and promoting successful reintegration. With its origins deeply rooted in the belief that everyone deserves a second chance, this program targets individuals who have faced challenges within the criminal justice system and are seeking a new path.

At the core of the First Chance Program lies its comprehensive approach, which encompasses a range of components designed to address the multifaceted needs of participants. From educational opportunities to vocational training and mental health support, this program leaves no stone unturned in equipping individuals with the tools they need to rebuild their lives.

The impact of the First Chance Program is undeniable. Through its holistic approach, it has not only significantly reduced recidivism rates but has also provided a platform for successful reintegration. By addressing the underlying issues that often contribute to criminal behavior, this program empowers individuals to break free from the cycle of crime and embrace a future filled with hope and possibility.

Case Study 2: The Second Chance Initiative

The Second Chance Initiative has emerged as a beacon of hope for individuals seeking to turn their lives around after incarceration. By providing a comprehensive range of services and support, this program aims to facilitate a smooth transition back into society and empower participants to become productive citizens.

With a focus on serving specific communities, the Second Chance Initiative recognizes the importance of tailoring its approach to meet the unique needs of individuals within these contexts. Through a combination of educational programs, vocational training, and access to vital resources, this initiative seeks to bridge the gap between incarceration and successful reentry.

The effectiveness of the Second Chance Initiative is evident in the success stories that have emerged from its implementation. By empowering individuals to acquire the skills and knowledge necessary for self-sufficiency, this program has played a pivotal role in breaking the cycle of recidivism and fostering lasting positive change within communities.

Case Study 3: The Pathways to Redemption Project

The Pathways to Redemption Project takes a distinctive approach to restorative reentry, recognizing that true transformation requires more than just addressing external factors. Rooted in its core principles and values, this project places a strong emphasis on personal growth and inner healing.

By engaging participants in a range of activities and interventions, the Pathways to Redemption Project seeks to guide individuals towards a path of redemption and healing. From therapeutic interventions to restorative justice practices, this project creates an environment conducive to personal reflection and growth.

The impact of the Pathways to Redemption Project is profound. By fostering healing and instilling a sense of purpose and self-worth, this program has helped individuals break free from the shackles of their past and embrace a future filled with hope and possibility. The transformation experienced by participants serves as a testament to the power of restorative reentry programs in facilitating holistic change.

Case Study 4: The Renewed Hope Program

The Renewed Hope Program has established itself as a trailblazer in the field of restorative reentry by adopting a comprehensive and multi-faceted approach. By recognizing the interconnectedness of educational, vocational, and mental health support, this program aims to equip individuals with the necessary tools to successfully reintegrate into society.

With a rich history of serving diverse populations, the Renewed Hope Program understands the importance of tailoring its services to meet the specific needs of each individual. By providing educational opportunities, vocational training, and mental health support, this program empowers participants to rebuild their lives and overcome the barriers they face.

The outcomes of the Renewed Hope Program speak for themselves. By reducing recidivism rates and promoting successful reintegration, this program has proven to be a catalyst for lasting positive change. Through its commitment to addressing the root causes of criminal behavior, the Renewed Hope Program offers individuals a renewed sense of purpose and hope for a brighter future.

Case Study 5: The Restorative Justice Initiative

The Restorative Justice Initiative takes a unique and transformative approach to restorative reentry by focusing on repairing harm, building empathy, and promoting accountability. This program recognizes that healing and growth are not solely the responsibility of individuals, but also the communities affected by crime.

Through its restorative practices, the Restorative Justice Initiative offers a platform for dialogue and reconciliation between individuals and their communities. By providing opportunities for healing and repair, this program aims to foster understanding and empathy while holding individuals accountable for their actions.

The impact of the Restorative Justice Initiative extends beyond the individual level. By promoting healing and rebuilding relationships, this program contributes to the overall well-being of communities affected by crime. Through its commitment to restorative practices, this initiative creates a path towards reconciliation and transformation.

Case Study 6: The Fresh Start Project

The Fresh Start Project is dedicated to providing individuals exiting the criminal justice system with the opportunities they need to rebuild their lives. With a mission rooted in empowerment and support, this program recognizes the importance of addressing the various barriers individuals face upon reentry.

By offering employment assistance, housing support, and mentorship, the Fresh Start Project equips participants with the necessary tools for stability and success. By focusing on holistic support, this program creates a foundation for individuals to overcome the challenges they encounter and build a brighter future.

The success of the Fresh Start Project lies in its ability to empower individuals to take control of their lives and create positive change. Through its comprehensive approach, this program has helped countless individuals achieve stability, find meaningful employment, and rebuild their lives.

Case Study 7: The Reentry Success Story Program

The Reentry Success Story Program takes an innovative approach to restorative reentry by harnessing the power of storytelling and personal narratives. This program recognizes that sharing personal experiences can inspire and empower both individuals with criminal records and the wider community.

By providing a platform for individuals to share their stories, the Reentry Success Story Program challenges stereotypes and fosters understanding and support for those seeking to rebuild their lives. By highlighting the resilience and determination of individuals, this program promotes empathy and breaks down the barriers that individuals with criminal records often face.

The impact of the Reentry Success Story Program extends far beyond the stories shared. By humanizing individuals with criminal records, this program contributes to a shift in societal attitudes and perceptions. Through its focus on storytelling, this program inspires others to embrace second chances and support individuals on their journey towards successful reintegration.

Case Study 8: The Community Connections Initiative

The Community Connections Initiative recognizes the vital role that community plays in the successful reintegration of individuals. By fostering connections and promoting community engagement, this program aims to create a support system that empowers individuals to rebuild their lives.

Through strategies such as volunteerism and collaboration, the Community Connections Initiative strengthens the bond between returning citizens and their communities. By providing opportunities for meaningful engagement, this program encourages social integration and helps individuals establish a sense of belonging.

The impact of the Community Connections Initiative is evident in the positive changes it brings to both individuals and communities. By facilitating connections and fostering a sense of community, this program contributes to the reduction of recidivism and the promotion of successful reintegration.

Case Study 9: The Restoration and Healing Project

The Restoration and Healing Project recognizes the importance of trauma-informed care and healing in the reentry process. This program takes a holistic approach, providing mental health support, counseling, and restorative justice practices to individuals as they reintegrate into society.

By prioritizing healing and resilience, the Restoration and Healing Project creates a safe and supportive environment for individuals to address the traumas they have experienced. By focusing on the individual's journey towards wholeness, this program equips participants with the necessary tools to navigate the challenges they may face.

The effectiveness of the Restoration and Healing Project lies in its ability to promote healing and facilitate successful reintegration. By recognizing the impact of trauma and providing support, this program empowers individuals to break free from the cycle of recidivism and embrace a future filled with restoration and hope.

Case Study 10: The Rebuilding Lives Initiative

The Rebuilding Lives Initiative takes a comprehensive approach to restorative reentry, recognizing that addressing the underlying causes of criminal behavior is crucial in fostering lasting positive change. By providing a range of services, such as substance abuse treatment, education, and job training, this program equips individuals with the tools they need to build meaningful and productive lives.

Through its commitment to comprehensive support, the Rebuilding Lives Initiative breaks the cycle of crime and provides individuals with the opportunity to create a brighter future. By addressing the root causes of criminal behavior, this program empowers individuals to overcome the barriers they face and embrace a life of purpose and fulfillment.

The impact of the Rebuilding Lives Initiative is far-reaching. By equipping individuals with the skills and resources they need to succeed, this program contributes to the reduction of recidivism and the promotion of successful reintegration. Through its comprehensive approach, the Rebuilding Lives Initiative offers individuals the chance to rewrite their stories and build lives filled with hope and possibility.

In summary, these case studies provide a glimpse into the transformative power of restorative reentry programs. By examining the origins, components, and outcomes of each program, we can gain valuable insights into the key factors that contribute to their success. From the First Chance Program to the Rebuilding Lives Initiative, these case studies demonstrate the diverse approaches and interventions employed to support individuals in their journey towards a brighter future. Through their collective impact, these programs offer hope, empowerment, and the opportunity for individuals to rebuild their lives and become productive members of society.

Overcoming Challenges

Introduction to Overcoming Challenges:

Implementing restorative practices during reentry can be a challenging process, filled with obstacles that may hinder progress. In this subchapter, we will address these common challenges head-on and explore strategies for overcoming them. It is crucial to understand the importance of overcoming these challenges in order to successfully implement restorative practices and achieve positive outcomes.

Understanding the Challenges:

During the reentry process, individuals face a myriad of challenges and obstacles that can impede their progress. These challenges range from social stigma and limited resources to emotional barriers and resistance to change. It is essential to identify and understand these challenges in order to effectively address them and navigate towards successful reentry. Additionally, we must also recognize the potential barriers that may hinder the implementation of restorative practices, such as lack of institutional support or inadequate training.

Challenges in Building Trust:

Building trust is a vital aspect of the reentry process, and it is also a specific challenge that individuals face. Trust between individuals is crucial for the effectiveness of restorative practices, as it creates a safe and supportive environment for healing and growth. However, trust can be difficult to establish, especially for those who have experienced trauma or have been let down by others in the past. It is important to explore strategies and techniques for building trust within the reentry process, such as active listening, open communication, and consistent support.

Overcoming Resistance to Change:

Resistance to change is a common challenge that can hinder the implementation of restorative practices. Many individuals may feel comfortable with their established routines or may be resistant to the idea of confronting past actions. Overcoming this resistance requires patience, empathy, and effective communication. It is essential to provide individuals with a clear understanding of the benefits of restorative practices and help them navigate their fears and anxieties surrounding change.

Navigating Power Dynamics:

Power dynamics within the reentry process can present significant challenges. These dynamics may stem from imbalances of power between different stakeholders or individuals within the reentry system. The success of restorative practices is heavily influenced by how power is distributed and managed. Navigating these dynamics requires open dialogue, transparent decision-making processes, and a commitment to equity and fairness.

Addressing Emotional Barriers:

Emotional barriers can significantly impact the implementation of restorative practices. Individuals in the reentry process may be dealing with a range of emotions, including shame, guilt, anger, or fear. These emotions can hinder their ability to fully engage in the restorative process. It is important to provide support and create a safe space for individuals to express and process their emotions. Techniques such as mindfulness, therapy, and peer support can be valuable tools in addressing and overcoming emotional barriers.

Dealing with Limited Resources:

Limited resources present a challenge when implementing restorative practices. These resources can include funding, staffing, or access to necessary services. However, it is important to find creative solutions and make the most of the available resources. Collaboration with community organizations, leveraging existing support systems, and exploring alternative funding sources can help overcome these challenges and ensure the successful implementation of restorative practices.

Supporting Stakeholder Engagement:

Engaging and involving all relevant stakeholders is crucial for the successful implementation of restorative practices. This includes individuals in the reentry process, community members, service providers, and policymakers. Fostering stakeholder engagement and collaboration requires effective communication, active participation, and a shared vision for restorative justice. Strategies such as regular meetings, workshops, and partnerships can facilitate stakeholder engagement and ensure a collective effort towards positive change.

Adapting to Individual Needs:

Each individual in the reentry process has unique needs that must be taken into account when implementing restorative practices. It is essential to tailor approaches and techniques to address these specific needs, whether it is providing trauma-informed care, culturally sensitive support, or individualized goal-setting. Adapting to individual needs ensures that restorative practices are inclusive, empowering, and effective.

Sustaining Restorative Practices:

Creating a sustainable and long-lasting restorative culture during reentry is a significant challenge. Restorative practices must be integrated into the fabric of the reentry system, rather than being treated as a temporary solution. This requires ongoing support, training, and evaluation to ensure their effectiveness over time. Strategies such as mentorship programs, peer support networks, and regular feedback loops can help sustain restorative practices and foster a culture of healing and growth.

By understanding and addressing these challenges, we can create a reentry process that embraces restorative practices and paves the way for successful reintegration into society. The journey may be difficult, but with perseverance, empathy, and a commitment to change, we can overcome these challenges and unlock the transformative power of restorative justice.

Key Takeaways

Introduction to Key Takeaways:

In writing my book Restorative Reentry, I've come to understand the importance of key takeaways in helping readers grasp and retain the main points of each chapter. Key takeaways serve as a summary of the main ideas presented, making it easier for readers to understand and apply the concepts discussed. By distilling complex information into concise and digestible points, key takeaways enhance the learning experience and empower readers to take action.

Identifying the Main Points:

One of the crucial steps in creating effective key takeaways is identifying the main points within a chapter. This process involves carefully analyzing the content to determine the core ideas and concepts being presented. By understanding the main points, readers gain a deeper comprehension of the material, enabling them to apply the knowledge more effectively in their own lives. It also helps in preventing information overload and allows for a more focused approach to learning.

Summarizing the Main Points:

Once the main points have been identified, the next step is summarizing them in a clear and concise manner. There are various techniques and strategies that can be employed for this purpose. Some may choose to highlight key ideas or concepts, while others might prefer using bullet points to succinctly present the main points. Regardless of the approach taken, the goal is to condense the information without losing its essence, providing readers with a concise summary that captures the essence of the chapter.

Organizing the Main Points:

Organizing the main points in a logical and coherent manner is essential for effective comprehension. By structuring the key takeaways in a way that flows smoothly, readers can easily follow the progression of ideas and concepts. This can be achieved through the use of subheadings or creating an outline that provides a clear structure for the main points. Organizing the key takeaways in this way ensures that readers can easily navigate the information and understand the connections between different concepts.

Creating a Concise Summary:

In order to create a concise summary of the main points, it is important to condense the information while still capturing its essence. This requires careful consideration of what is essential and what can be omitted without compromising the overall message. By distilling the main points into a concise summary, readers are able to grasp the core ideas more easily and quickly. This approach also allows for efficient review and revisiting of the main points in the future.

Ensuring Accuracy and Clarity:

Accuracy and clarity are paramount when presenting the main points in the key takeaways. It is important to convey the information in a way that is easily understandable by the reader, avoiding any ambiguity or confusion. By ensuring accuracy and clarity, readers can confidently apply the main points to their own lives and make informed decisions based on the knowledge presented in the book.

Providing Context:

Providing context for the main points is essential in enhancing their understanding and applicability. By offering background information or real-life examples, readers are able to connect the main points to their own experiences and gain a deeper appreciation for their relevance. Contextualizing the main points not only improves comprehension but also enables readers to see how the concepts can be practically applied in their own lives.

Highlighting Key Takeaways:

In order to help readers remember and apply the main points, it can be helpful to highlight key takeaways within the summary. This could involve using bold or italicized text to draw attention to the most important concepts or ideas. By emphasizing these key takeaways, readers are more likely to retain the core messages of the chapter and apply them to their own lives.

Applying the Main Points:

The main points presented in each chapter of Restorative Reentry are not meant to be simply theoretical concepts, but rather actionable tools that can be applied in real-life situations. By understanding and applying the main points, readers can solve problems, make informed decisions, and ultimately improve their lives. It is through the application of these main points that true transformation and growth can occur.

Reviewing and Revisiting the Main Points:

To ensure better understanding and retention, it is important for readers to review and revisit the main points presented in each chapter. This can be done through various strategies, such as creating flashcards or discussing the main points with others. By regularly reviewing and revisiting the main points, readers reinforce their understanding and deepen their knowledge, allowing them to fully integrate the concepts into their lives.

In conclusion, key takeaways play a crucial role in enhancing the learning experience for readers of Restorative Reentry. By identifying, summarizing, organizing, and highlighting the main points, readers are empowered to understand and apply the concepts presented in each chapter. With accuracy, clarity, and context, the main points become valuable tools that can be applied to real-life situations. Through regular review and revisiting, readers solidify their understanding and ensure long-term retention. The key takeaways are not just a summary of the content, but a roadmap for personal growth and transformation.

Resources for Further Learning

Introduction to Resources for Further Learning:

In this subchapter, I want to offer readers a wealth of resources, books, and organizations that can help deepen their understanding of restorative justice. It's important to recognize that learning is an ongoing process, and embracing the principles and practices of restorative justice requires continued growth and expansion of knowledge. By providing these additional resources, I hope to empower readers to dive deeper into this field and become active participants in the restorative justice movement.

Recommended Books:

There are several books that I highly recommend for those who are interested in delving deeper into the topic of restorative justice. These books offer in-depth explorations of the principles and practices of restorative justice, and provide valuable insights for readers. Here are a few notable recommendations:

1. "The Little Book of Restorative Justice" by Howard Zehr: This book serves as an excellent introduction to the concept of restorative justice. Zehr, a renowned expert in the field, provides a concise yet comprehensive overview of the principles and applications of restorative justice. Readers can expect to gain a clear understanding of the underlying philosophy and learn practical ways to implement restorative justice in their own lives.

2. "Restorative Justice: Healing the Foundations of Our Everyday Lives" by Mark Umbreit: Umbreit's book offers a holistic perspective on restorative justice, exploring its potential to transform not only the criminal justice system but also other aspects of our daily lives. Through thought-provoking stories and real-life examples, Umbreit demonstrates how restorative justice can foster healing and reconciliation in various contexts. Readers will gain a deeper understanding of the transformative power of restorative justice.

Online Resources:

The internet has become a treasure trove of information, and there are several online platforms and websites that offer valuable resources on restorative justice. These resources can be accessed easily and provide a wealth of knowledge. Here are a few noteworthy online resources:

1. Restorative Justice Online: This website serves as a comprehensive hub for all things related to restorative justice. It offers a vast array of articles, research papers, and case studies, providing readers with a thorough understanding of the subject. The website also features discussion forums where individuals can engage in meaningful conversations and share insights on restorative justice.

2. Restorative Practices International: This online platform offers a range of resources, including webinars, podcasts, and training materials. It provides a space for individuals to learn from experts in the field and gain practical skills in implementing restorative justice. The platform's user-friendly interface and interactive features make it an invaluable resource for

those seeking to deepen their understanding of restorative justice.

Educational Programs:

For individuals who are looking to engage in a more structured learning experience, there are several educational programs and courses that focus on restorative justice. These programs provide a structured curriculum and cover a wide range of topics. Here are a few notable educational programs:

1. The International Institute for Restorative Practices (IIRP): This institute offers a variety of courses and programs, ranging from introductory workshops to advanced certifications. The programs cover topics such as restorative practices in schools, workplaces, and communities. Participants can expect to gain practical skills and knowledge that can be applied in their respective fields.

2. Center for Justice and Reconciliation: This organization offers an online course on restorative justice, providing participants with a comprehensive understanding of the principles and practices. The course covers topics such as victim-offender dialogue, circle processes, and restorative justice in the criminal justice system. Participants will have the opportunity to learn from experts in the field and engage in meaningful discussions with fellow learners.

Training Workshops:

Attending training workshops can be a transformative experience for individuals seeking to gain practical skills and knowledge in restorative justice. These workshops offer hands-on learning opportunities and provide a platform for individuals to connect with like-minded individuals. Here are a few benefits of attending training workshops:

1. Practical Skills: Training workshops provide participants with the opportunity to learn practical skills in restorative justice, such as facilitation techniques and circle processes. These skills can be applied in various contexts, including schools, workplaces, and community settings.

2. Networking: Training workshops bring together individuals who are passionate about restorative justice, providing a platform for networking and collaboration. Participants have the opportunity to connect with experts in the field, share insights, and build meaningful relationships.

Professional Organizations:

Professional organizations play a crucial role in promoting restorative justice and providing resources for further learning. These organizations offer a range of benefits, including access to exclusive resources, networking opportunities, and professional development. Here are a few notable professional organizations:

1. The Restorative Justice Council: This organization is dedicated to promoting restorative justice across various sectors, including criminal justice, education, and community settings. Members of the organization gain access to a range of resources, including research articles, case studies, and training materials. The

organization also offers networking opportunities and organizes events to facilitate knowledge exchange.

2. International Institute for Restorative Practices (IIRP): In addition to its educational programs, the IIRP also serves as a professional organization that provides ongoing support to individuals working in the field of restorative justice. Members gain access to a community of practitioners, as well as resources such as webinars, research articles, and toolkits.

Webinars and Podcasts:

Webinars and podcasts offer valuable insights and discussions on restorative justice, making them an excellent resource for further learning. Here are a few webinars and podcasts that provide insightful discussions on restorative justice:

1. "Restorative Justice Now" podcast: This podcast features interviews with experts in the field of restorative justice, offering listeners a chance to gain insights from experienced practitioners. The episodes cover a wide range of topics, including the implementation of restorative justice in different contexts and the impact of restorative justice on communities.

2. "Restorative Justice Webinar Series" by Restorative Justice Online: This webinar series features presentations by leading scholars and practitioners in the field of restorative justice. The webinars cover various topics, including restorative justice in schools, the intersection of restorative justice and mental health, and the role of restorative justice in addressing systemic injustices.

Academic Research and Journals:

Academic research and journals play a crucial role in deepening our understanding of restorative justice. These resources provide in-depth analysis and insights into the field, and offer opportunities for further exploration. Here are a few academic journals that focus on restorative justice:

1. The International Journal of Restorative Justice: This peer-reviewed journal publishes research articles, case studies, and theoretical analyses on restorative justice. It covers a wide range of topics, including the implementation of restorative justice in different contexts, the impact of restorative justice on victims and offenders, and the role of restorative justice in addressing social inequalities.

2. Restorative Justice: An International Journal: This journal publishes interdisciplinary research on restorative justice, exploring its applications in various settings, such as criminal justice, education, and community development. The articles provide valuable insights and contribute to the ongoing dialogue surrounding restorative justice.

Community-Based Organizations:

Community-based organizations play a vital role in promoting restorative justice at the grassroots level. These organizations offer a range of resources and initiatives that individuals can get involved in to further their understanding of restorative justice. Here are a few examples of community-based organizations:

1. Restorative Justice for Oakland Youth (RJOY): This organization focuses on implementing restorative justice practices in schools and communities in Oakland, California. RJOY offers training programs, coaching services, and consultation to schools and community organizations. Individuals can get involved by volunteering or participating in their community events.

2. Community Justice for Youth Institute: This organization works with communities across the United States to implement restorative justice practices in addressing youth crime and conflict. They offer training programs, technical assistance, and resources for communities seeking to embrace restorative justice approaches. Individuals can engage with the organization by participating in their community initiatives or volunteering.

International Organizations and Networks:

International organizations and networks play a vital role in fostering collaboration and knowledge exchange on restorative justice at a global level. These organizations bring together individuals and organizations from different countries, providing opportunities for cross-cultural learning and collaboration. Here are a few international organizations and networks:

1. International Institute for Restorative Practices (IIRP): In addition to its educational programs, the IIRP also serves as an international organization that fosters collaboration and exchange of knowledge on restorative justice. The organization hosts conferences, facilitates international partnerships, and offers resources for

individuals and organizations working in the field of restorative justice.

2. Restorative Justice International: This global network brings together individuals and organizations committed to promoting restorative justice worldwide. The network offers resources, training programs, and facilitates knowledge exchange through conferences and events. Individuals can engage with the network by participating in their initiatives or becoming members.

By providing these resources, books, and organizations, I aim to equip readers with the tools they need to deepen their understanding of restorative justice and become active participants in the restorative justice movement. Through continued learning and exploration, individuals can make a significant impact in promoting healing, reconciliation, and social justice within their communities and beyond.

Discussion Questions

Introduction and Problem Statement:

As I embarked on writing this book, Restorative Reentry, I quickly realized the importance of thought-provoking questions in engaging readers. I believe that asking the right questions can spark curiosity and encourage readers to dive deeper into the subject matter. Reflection and discussion are powerful tools that can enhance understanding and critical thinking skills, leading to personal growth and transformation. In this subchapter, I aim to present discussion questions that will prompt readers to reflect on their own experiences and engage in meaningful conversations.

The Power of Thought-Provoking Questions:

Thought-provoking questions have the ability to stimulate curiosity and deepen comprehension. By posing challenging questions, readers are compelled to think critically and explore different perspectives. These questions have the potential to ignite insightful discussions, fostering a collaborative learning environment. Throughout history, thought-provoking questions have sparked intellectual debates and led to groundbreaking discoveries. Take, for example, Socrates' question, "What is the meaning of life?" This simple question has been pondered by philosophers and thinkers for centuries, opening up a world of possibilities and inviting individuals to contemplate their own existence.

The Types of Discussion Questions:

There are different types of discussion questions that can be used to encourage reflection and dialogue. Open-ended questions, for instance, invite readers to delve deeper into a topic by offering their own insights and interpretations. Hypothetical questions challenge readers to imagine different scenarios and consider alternative outcomes. Controversial questions push readers to explore conflicting viewpoints and engage in thoughtful debates. Each type of question has its advantages and disadvantages, and it is important to use them strategically to stimulate meaningful reflection and discussion. For example, open-ended questions allow for more creative thinking, while controversial questions may create tension but also encourage critical analysis.

Designing Effective Discussion Questions:

Creating thought-provoking questions requires careful consideration. First and foremost, it is crucial to think about the target audience and the specific context of the reading material. Questions should be tailored to their needs and interests. Clarity is essential, ensuring that the questions are easily understood and can be interpreted in different ways. Relevance is another important factor to consider. Questions should be directly related to the topic at hand, allowing readers to make connections and apply their knowledge. Finally, diversity in the questions is crucial, as it encourages readers to think from various perspectives and broadens their understanding of the subject matter.

Applying Discussion Questions to Texts:

Incorporating discussion questions into various types of reading materials, such as books, articles, and essays, can greatly enhance the learning experience. These questions act as a guide, encouraging readers to analyze and interpret the texts in a deeper and more meaningful way. By engaging with the material through discussion, readers are able to share their thoughts, gain new insights, and challenge their own beliefs. The benefits of using discussion questions as a teaching or learning tool are immeasurable, as they promote active engagement and encourage critical thinking skills.

Promoting Reflection and Discussion:

Facilitating reflection and discussion among readers requires creating a safe and inclusive environment. As the author or facilitator, it is important to establish trust and encourage open dialogue. Providing guidelines for respectful communication and actively listening to participants' perspectives is crucial. Moderators play a vital role in guiding the conversation, ensuring that all voices are heard and encouraging active participation. By promoting reflection and discussion, readers are empowered to share their thoughts, engage in respectful dialogue, and learn from one another's experiences.

Assessing Learning and Understanding:

Assessing readers' learning and understanding through reflection and discussion is a key component of this process. It is important to evaluate the effectiveness of the discussion questions in order to improve future iterations. This can be done through surveys or group assessments, allowing readers to provide feedback on their experience. Assessing learning and understanding provides valuable insights into the impact of the discussion questions and helps identify areas for improvement. By continuously assessing and adapting, we can ensure that the questions we pose are effective in fostering growth and transformation.

Implementing Discussion Questions in Different Settings:

Discussion questions can be implemented in various settings, such as classrooms, book clubs, or online forums. Each setting presents its own unique challenges and considerations. In a classroom, for example, it is important to create a structured environment that encourages active participation from all students. In a book club, discussions may be more informal, allowing for a deeper exploration of individual interpretations. Online forums provide the opportunity for a wider audience to engage in discussions, but may require additional moderation to ensure respectful dialogue. Examples of successful implementation of discussion questions in real-world contexts can inspire and guide readers in applying these techniques in their own settings.

In conclusion, thought-provoking questions are powerful tools that can engage readers, stimulate critical thinking, and promote personal growth. By incorporating discussion questions into our reading materials and facilitating reflection and dialogue, we can create transformative learning experiences. It is important to design effective questions, consider the specific context and target audience, and promote an inclusive and respectful environment. Assessing learning and understanding allows for continuous improvement, and implementing discussion questions in different settings opens up opportunities for meaningful engagement. So, let's embark on this journey of restorative reentry together, armed with thought-provoking questions that will challenge us to reflect, discuss, and grow.

Chapter 3: Healing From Trauma

Understanding Trauma

Introduction and Overview:

Understanding trauma is essential in the field of psychology and mental health. In this subchapter, we will delve into the significance of trauma and its effects on individuals. By examining the different types of trauma and their impact, we can gain a deeper understanding of the complexities of trauma and its role in shaping our psychological and emotional well-being.

Definition and Explanation of Trauma:

Trauma is not just a buzzword; it holds immense significance when it comes to our psychological and emotional well-being. At its core, trauma refers to any deeply distressing or disturbing experience that overwhelms our ability to cope. It can result from a wide range of factors, including abuse, neglect, accidents, or natural disasters. The effects of trauma can be immediate and long-lasting, leaving a profound impact on individuals' lives.

Types of Trauma:

To fully grasp the complexity of trauma, we must explore its different types. Acute trauma refers to a single traumatic event, such as a car accident or a physical assault. Chronic trauma, on the other hand, involves repeated exposure to distressing events, such as ongoing abuse or witnessing violence. Complex trauma refers to multiple and varied traumatic experiences, often occurring within interpersonal relationships. Lastly, secondary trauma refers to the indirect exposure to trauma, such as hearing about traumatic events or working with trauma survivors. Each type of trauma carries its own characteristics and unique aspects, shaping individuals' experiences in distinct ways.

Emotional and Psychological Effects of Trauma:

The emotional and psychological effects of trauma can be overwhelming. Post-traumatic stress disorder (PTSD) is a well-known consequence of trauma, characterized by intrusive memories, nightmares, and hypervigilance. Anxiety and depression are also commonly experienced by individuals who have endured trauma, as well as dissociation, a disconnection from oneself and reality. These effects can erode an individual's self-esteem, strain relationships, and diminish overall quality of life.

Physical Effects of Trauma:

While the psychological impacts of trauma are often discussed, it is important not to overlook its physical effects. Trauma can disrupt sleep patterns, leading to insomnia or nightmares. Changes in appetite and weight are also common. Moreover, trauma has a profound impact on the immune system, potentially leading to increased vulnerability to illness and a compromised ability to fight off infections. In fact, trauma has been linked to various physical health issues, including chronic pain, cardiovascular problems, and autoimmune disorders.

Cognitive Effects of Trauma:

Trauma doesn't just affect our emotions and physical health; it also takes a toll on our cognitive functioning. Difficulties with memory, attention, concentration, and decision-making are all common cognitive effects of trauma. This can have a significant impact on an individual's ability to trust, problem-solve, and engage in future-oriented thinking. The cognitive effects of trauma can make it challenging for individuals to navigate their daily lives and plan for the future.

Social and Interpersonal Effects of Trauma:

Trauma can have far-reaching effects on an individual's social and interpersonal relationships. Difficulties with trust, intimacy, and forming healthy connections are commonly experienced by trauma survivors. The potential for social isolation is also heightened, as individuals may withdraw from social activities and relationships due to fear and shame. Communication and boundary-setting can become challenging, leading to strained relationships and an increased sense of isolation.

Impact on Development and Attachment:

Trauma has a profound impact on an individual's development, particularly when experienced in childhood. The effects of trauma can disrupt normal developmental processes, including attachment styles, emotional regulation, and the overall development of a sense of self. This can result in difficulties forming healthy relationships and navigating the world as adults. Understanding the impact of trauma on development is crucial in order to provide appropriate support and interventions for individuals who have experienced trauma.

Resilience and Post-Traumatic Growth:

Despite the devastating effects of trauma, it is important to recognize the potential for resilience and post-traumatic growth. Resilience refers to the ability to bounce back and recover from adversity, and many individuals demonstrate remarkable resilience in the face of trauma. Moreover, trauma can lead to personal growth and positive change. Post-traumatic growth is a concept that acknowledges the potential for individuals to find meaning, develop new perspectives, and experience personal growth following trauma. Recognizing and fostering resilience and post-traumatic growth is essential in promoting healing and restoration after trauma.

Understanding Trauma in a Cultural Context:

Trauma cannot be fully understood without considering the cultural context in which it occurs. Cultural factors play a significant role in shaping individuals' experiences and expressions of trauma. They also influence the availability of support and resources for trauma survivors. Cultural beliefs, values, and norms can impact how trauma is perceived and how individuals seek help and support. Taking into account cultural context is crucial in providing effective and culturally sensitive interventions for trauma survivors.

By delving into the definition, types, effects, and cultural context of trauma, we can gain a comprehensive understanding of its impact on individuals. This exploration will serve as a foundation for the subsequent chapters, which will focus on strategies and interventions for healing and restoration in the aftermath of trauma.

Healing Modalities

When it comes to the recovery process, healing modalities play a crucial role in restoring one's well-being and achieving a sense of wholeness. In this chapter, we will explore various healing modalities and their significance in the journey of restoration.

Therapy, as a healing modality, holds immense power in aiding recovery. It provides individuals with a safe space to explore their emotions, thoughts, and experiences. Different types of therapy, such as cognitive-behavioral therapy and psychoanalysis, offer unique approaches to healing. Cognitive-behavioral therapy helps individuals identify and change negative thought patterns and behaviors, while psychoanalysis delves deep into the subconscious to uncover underlying causes of distress. Through therapy, individuals can gain valuable insights, develop coping mechanisms, and build resilience on their recovery journey.

Mindfulness is another powerful healing modality that can greatly contribute to one's recovery process. Mindfulness, defined as being fully present and aware of one's thoughts, feelings, and sensations, allows individuals to cultivate self-awareness and cope with stress. By practicing mindfulness, individuals can learn to observe their thoughts and emotions without judgment, enabling them to respond to challenges in a more calm and constructive manner. Techniques such as meditation, deep breathing, and body scans can be utilized to cultivate mindfulness and enhance the recovery experience.

Art, in all its forms, has long been recognized as a therapeutic modality that promotes self-expression and emotional healing. Engaging in artistic activities can provide individuals with a means of communication that transcends words. Painting, writing, music, and other art forms allow individuals to tap into their creativity and express their emotions in a safe and non-verbal manner. Through art, individuals can explore their inner worlds, process trauma, and find solace and healing.

Alternative healing modalities, such as acupuncture, yoga, and herbal medicine, offer additional avenues for recovery. These modalities have been used for centuries in various cultures and have shown promising results in aiding healing. While the benefits of alternative healing modalities may vary for each individual, they can provide a holistic approach to recovery by addressing physical, emotional, and spiritual well-being. Stories of individuals who have found success in using these modalities serve as a testament to their potential effectiveness.

Integrative approaches to healing, which combine multiple healing modalities, can provide a comprehensive and well-rounded recovery experience. By integrating therapy, mindfulness, art, and other modalities, individuals can benefit from the synergistic effects of these practices. This holistic approach addresses the multidimensional aspects of recovery, enhancing overall well-being and facilitating long-term healing. Programs and therapies that have successfully integrated different modalities serve as inspiring examples of the power of an integrative approach.

While healing modalities offer immense potential for recovery, it is important to address the challenges and criticisms associated with them. Some argue against the effectiveness of healing modalities due to the lack of scientific evidence or empirical support. It is essential to acknowledge these concerns and promote evidence-based practices to ensure the efficacy of healing modalities. Additionally, individuals may face limitations or challenges when utilizing healing modalities, such as financial constraints, lack of accessibility, or personal resistance to change. Recognizing and addressing these challenges is crucial in supporting individuals on their recovery journey.

Research studies and evidence play a vital role in supporting the effectiveness of healing modalities. Numerous studies have shown positive outcomes in using therapy, mindfulness, and art in the recovery process. These findings validate the importance of integrating healing modalities into traditional approaches to recovery. It is essential to prioritize evidence-based practices in the field of healing modalities to ensure the highest quality of care and outcomes for individuals seeking recovery.

Personal testimonials and success stories further highlight the transformative power of healing modalities. Individuals who have benefited from therapy, mindfulness, and art share their stories of growth, resilience, and improved well-being. These testimonials serve as a source of inspiration and encouragement for others who may be embarking on their own recovery journey. They showcase the potential of healing modalities to help individuals overcome challenges, rediscover themselves, and live fulfilling lives.

The role of professionals in implementing healing modalities cannot be understated. Trained therapists, mindfulness instructors, and art therapists play a crucial role in guiding individuals through the recovery process. Their expertise and support ensure a safe and effective utilization of healing modalities. By working closely with qualified practitioners, individuals can maximize the benefits of healing modalities and navigate their recovery journey with professional guidance.

In conclusion, healing modalities such as therapy, mindfulness, and art offer powerful tools for individuals seeking restoration and recovery. By incorporating these modalities into their lives, individuals can tap into their inner strength, cultivate self-awareness, and embark on a transformative journey of healing. It is my hope that readers will explore and utilize these modalities to enhance their own recovery and well-being, embracing the potential for growth and restoration that lies within them.

Building Resilience

I'd like to share a personal testimonial to provide a real-life example of building resilience during the challenges of reentry. The purpose of this subchapter is to offer strategies for developing resilience and coping skills in the context of reentry. It's important to understand that reentry after a period of incarceration can be incredibly daunting, with numerous obstacles to overcome. By sharing this testimonial, I hope to shed light on the journey of someone who has experienced reentry and demonstrate how they built resilience throughout the process.

Let me introduce you to John. After serving a period of incarceration, John faced significant challenges upon reentering society. Finding employment proved to be one of the most difficult obstacles. Many employers were hesitant to hire someone with a criminal record, making it incredibly discouraging for John to secure a job. Rebuilding relationships was also a struggle for John. He faced judgment and stigma from friends and family, making it difficult to regain their trust and rebuild those connections. Adjusting to a new routine and a completely different environment further tested his resilience during this process.

Throughout his reentry journey, John encountered specific moments and experiences that truly put his resilience and coping skills to the test. For instance, when he was rejected from numerous job applications, it was easy for him to feel defeated and give up. However, John chose to view these rejections as opportunities to improve himself and his skills. He sought out additional training and education, demonstrating his determination to overcome the challenges he faced.

Reflecting on John's journey, it is clear that his resilience played a vital role in his successful reentry. He utilized various strategies and coping mechanisms to navigate the obstacles he encountered. For example, John actively engaged in positive self-talk and surrounded himself with a supportive network of individuals who believed in his potential. These strategies not only helped him maintain a positive mindset but also provided the necessary encouragement and motivation to keep pushing forward.

In analyzing the effectiveness of these strategies, it becomes evident that they were successful in building resilience because they focused on developing a positive mindset, setting goals, and establishing a support network. These are principles of resilience that can be applied to any reentry process. By adopting a positive mindset, individuals can shift their perspective and approach challenges with a solution-oriented mindset. Setting goals provides a sense of direction and purpose, serving as a source of motivation and focus. Lastly, developing a support network ensures that individuals have a strong support system to rely on during difficult times.

Building coping skills is crucial during reentry, and there are several practical strategies that can be implemented. Engaging in self-care activities such as exercise, meditation, and journaling can help individuals manage stress and improve overall well-being. Additionally, learning to identify and manage emotions in a healthy way is essential for coping effectively. By developing these coping skills, individuals can navigate the challenges of reentry with greater resilience and emotional well-being.

Navigating challenges during reentry can be overwhelming, but it's important to address them head-on. Specific challenges such as finding stable housing or dealing with stigma require strategic approaches. Seeking support from community organizations and developing a support system of friends and family can provide individuals with the necessary resources and encouragement to overcome these obstacles. Resilience plays a significant role in maintaining a positive mindset throughout these challenges.

Building social connections is an essential aspect of the reentry process. Establishing new relationships and rebuilding existing ones can provide individuals with a sense of belonging and support. Joining support groups or engaging in community activities can offer opportunities for social connection and growth.

Problem-solving skills are another important component of building resilience during reentry. Developing effective problem-solving skills, such as breaking down problems into manageable steps and seeking advice from trusted individuals, can contribute to a sense of empowerment and resilience. By actively engaging in problem-solving, individuals gain confidence in their ability to overcome obstacles and adapt to new circumstances.

It's important to acknowledge that building resilience during reentry can be challenging, and seeking professional help is a valid option. There are numerous resources and organizations that offer support for individuals going through the reentry process.

Encouraging individuals to reach out for professional assistance when needed is crucial in ensuring their well-being and continued growth.

Lastly, it's essential to view resilience as an ongoing process of growth and development. Reentry presents an opportunity for personal growth, and individuals must remain committed to building resilience even after overcoming initial obstacles. Continuous self-reflection, learning, and adapting to new challenges are key components of this process. By embracing this mindset, individuals can continue to thrive and develop resilience in all areas of their lives.

In conclusion, developing resilience and coping skills during the reentry process is crucial for individuals seeking to successfully reintegrate into society. Through the testimonial of John's journey, we have seen firsthand the challenges he faced and the strategies he utilized to build resilience. By focusing on positive mindset, goal-setting, developing a support network, engaging in self-care activities, and building problem-solving skills, individuals can navigate the challenges of reentry with resilience and improve their overall well-being. Seeking professional help when needed and viewing resilience as an ongoing process of growth and development are also important aspects of the reentry journey.

Support Systems

When it comes to healing and recovering from a traumatic event, support systems play a crucial role in our journey. They provide the foundation on which we can rebuild our lives, offering comfort, guidance, and understanding. In the following paragraphs, I want to share a personal testimonial that exemplifies the significance of supportive relationships and community networks in the healing process.

Let me introduce you to Sarah. Sarah was a vibrant and independent woman who experienced a devastating car accident that left her physically and emotionally scarred. In the beginning, she felt overwhelmed by the challenges she faced. She struggled with daily activities, faced isolation, and battled with depression. However, Sarah realized that she couldn't go through this healing journey alone. She actively sought out support from others, recognizing the importance of leaning on loved ones during difficult times.

Sarah's support system consisted of her immediate family, close friends, and a support group specifically for survivors of trauma. Her family was there every step of the way, providing emotional support, assisting with everyday tasks, and encouraging her to seek professional help. Sarah's friends, too, played a significant role, offering a listening ear, spending quality time with her, and reminding her of her strength and resilience. The support group became a safe space for Sarah to connect with others who had experienced similar traumas, allowing her to share her story, gain validation, and learn from their journeys.

The different forms of support Sarah received were instrumental in her healing process. Emotionally, her support system provided a sense of belonging and validation, reminding her that she was not alone in her struggles. Practically, they offered assistance with transportation, meal preparation, and even accompanied her to therapy sessions. Additionally, her community network helped connect her with resources such as support services, counseling, and rehabilitation programs, which were vital in her recovery.

The impact that these supportive relationships and community networks had on Sarah's healing journey cannot be understated. They provided a lifeline of hope, compassion, and strength during her darkest moments. With their unwavering support, Sarah was able to find the resilience within herself to face the challenges head-on and embrace the healing process. She no longer felt alone but surrounded by a network of love and care.

Reflecting on Sarah's story, we can draw valuable insights into the importance of having a strong support system during times of healing and recovery. Supportive relationships and community networks offer a sense of belonging, validation, and understanding that are crucial for our emotional well-being. They serve as pillars of strength and resilience, helping us navigate the obstacles that come our way.

However, accessing support systems may not always be easy. Barriers such as stigma, lack of awareness, or geographical distance can hinder individuals from reaching out for help. In Restorative Reentry, we will explore strategies for overcoming these challenges and creating a supportive environment that fosters healing and growth.

Reciprocal support is another crucial aspect of support systems. While receiving support is vital, offering support to others can also have profound benefits for both the giver and the receiver. It creates a sense of community, empathy, and interconnectedness, reinforcing the notion that healing is a collective journey.

Connecting Sarah's testimonial to broader themes, we see how supportive relationships and community networks can complement professional support and therapy. They provide a unique form of care and understanding that professionals may not always be able to offer. By working together, these various support systems can create a safe and inclusive environment where healing can thrive.

Moreover, the long-term effects of having a strong support system are remarkable. It not only aids in the recovery process but also enhances overall well-being and resilience. By fostering and maintaining supportive relationships and community networks, individuals can cultivate a foundation of support that will continue to nurture their growth and healing for years to come.

In conclusion, Sarah's journey exemplifies the transformative power of support systems in the healing process. By embracing the love and care of her family, friends, and support group, she was able to overcome her challenges, find resilience, and experience personal growth. Let Sarah's testimonial be a reminder of the importance of surrounding ourselves with a strong support system as we navigate our own healing journeys.

Self-Care Practices

Introduction to Self-Care Practices

Taking care of ourselves is crucial for our overall well-being and self-empowerment. In this subchapter, I will provide you with practical techniques for self-care that you can incorporate into your daily routine. By prioritizing self-care, we can enhance our physical, mental, emotional, and spiritual health, ultimately leading to a more fulfilling and empowered life.

The Science behind Self-Care

Self-care practices are not just some trendy buzzwords; they have a scientific basis that supports their effectiveness. Numerous studies have shown the positive effects of self-care on our mental and physical health. Engaging in self-care activities triggers the release of endorphins, which are our body's natural feel-good chemicals. These activities also reduce stress hormones, lower blood pressure, and boost our immune system. By understanding the scientific evidence behind self-care, we can fully embrace its importance and incorporate it into our lives.

Physical Self-Care Techniques

Physical self-care is essential for maintaining our overall well-being. Engaging in regular exercise, eating a balanced diet, and getting adequate sleep are crucial practices to prioritize. Exercise not only strengthens our bodies but also releases endorphins, improving our mood and reducing stress. Eating nutritious meals provides our bodies with the necessary fuel for optimal functioning. And getting enough sleep ensures that we have the energy and focus to tackle each day with vitality. By incorporating these physical self-care techniques, we can enhance our well-being and feel empowered in our bodies.

Mental and Emotional Self-Care Techniques

Taking care of our mental and emotional health is equally important. Mindfulness, stress management, and therapy are effective techniques to prioritize. Mindfulness practices, such as meditation or deep breathing exercises, help us stay present and reduce anxiety. Stress management techniques, such as journaling or engaging in relaxing activities, help us cope with the demands of daily life. Therapy provides a safe space for us to explore and address any underlying emotional issues. By implementing these mental and emotional self-care techniques, we can cultivate a greater sense of well-being and emotional resilience.

Social Self-Care Techniques

Building and maintaining healthy relationships and setting boundaries are essential for our social well-being. Nurturing our connections with others through regular social interactions and quality time spent with loved ones is crucial for our sense of belonging and support. Setting healthy boundaries ensures that we prioritize our own needs and protect our emotional well-being. By incorporating these social self-care techniques, we can foster a strong support system and feel empowered within our relationships.

Creative Self-Care Techniques

Engaging in creative activities is a powerful form of self-care. Whether it's painting, writing, playing an instrument, or any other artistic pursuit, these activities foster self-expression and personal fulfillment. They provide an outlet for our emotions and allow us to tap into our innate creativity. By embracing these creative self-care techniques, we can cultivate a deeper connection with ourselves and find joy in our creative endeavors.

Spiritual Self-Care Techniques

Nurturing our spiritual well-being is essential for finding purpose and connection to something greater. Engaging in spiritual practices such as meditation, prayer, or connecting with nature can help us cultivate a sense of inner peace and alignment. These practices provide us with a deeper understanding of ourselves and the world around us. By incorporating these spiritual self-care techniques, we can find solace, meaning, and a greater sense of purpose in our lives.

Self-Care for Work-Life Balance

Maintaining a healthy work-life balance is crucial for our overall well-being. Prioritizing self-care practices specifically tailored for this balance is essential. Setting boundaries between work and personal life, taking regular breaks, and engaging in activities that bring us joy outside of work are all important aspects of self-care in the workplace. By implementing these self-care practices, we can prevent burnout, enhance our productivity, and find satisfaction in both our personal and professional lives.

Self-Care in Challenging Times

During challenging situations or stressors, self-care becomes even more crucial. Engaging in self-care techniques that build resilience and aid in emotional well-being is vital. Practices such as practicing gratitude, seeking support from loved ones, or engaging in self-reflection can help us navigate difficult times with strength and grace. By prioritizing self-care during challenging periods, we can build resilience and maintain our emotional well-being.

Developing a Personalized Self-Care Plan

Developing a personalized self-care plan is an essential step in incorporating self-care into our lives. By tailoring self-care practices to our individual needs and preferences, we ensure that they are sustainable and effective. Take the time to reflect on what activities bring you joy, what practices nourish your mind and body, and what rituals connect you to something greater. Create a self-care plan that is unique to you, and commit to prioritizing it. By developing a personalized self-care plan, we can embark on a journey of self-empowerment and well-being.

Reframing the Narrative

Introduction to Reframing the Narrative

Reframing the narrative is a powerful concept that can have a profound impact on our self-image and overall well-being. It involves shifting our perspective and redefining our identity in a positive light. In a society that often emphasizes our past mistakes and shortcomings, reframing the narrative allows us to break free from the chains of negative self-perception and cultivate a more positive and empowering self-image.

Our past mistakes can have a significant impact on how we view ourselves. We may internalize those mistakes and allow them to define us, leading to feelings of shame, guilt, and low self-worth. However, it's essential to acknowledge that mistakes are a natural part of the growth process. They do not define who we are as individuals, but rather serve as opportunities for learning and personal development.

Identifying negative self-beliefs is a crucial step in reframing the narrative. These beliefs act as barriers to our personal growth and contribute to a negative self-image. They may manifest as thoughts such as "I'm not good enough," "I always mess things up," or "I don't deserve happiness." These beliefs hold us back from reaching our full potential and can have a detrimental impact on various aspects of our lives, including relationships, career, and overall well-being.

Challenging and reframing negative self-beliefs is key to cultivating a positive self-image. This involves questioning the validity of these beliefs and replacing them with more empowering and accurate thoughts. Self-reflection and self-awareness play vital roles in this process. By examining our thoughts and beliefs, we can gain a deeper understanding of how they shape our self-perception and take steps to challenge and reframe them.

Shifting our focus to the positive aspects of ourselves is an essential part of reframing the narrative. We all have unique qualities, strengths, and achievements that often go unnoticed or overshadowed by our mistakes. By intentionally identifying and acknowledging these positive aspects, we can build a more positive self-image. Focusing on our strengths and achievements allows us to see ourselves in a more empowering light and boosts our confidence and self-esteem.

Cultivating self-compassion is another crucial aspect of reframing the narrative. Often, we are our own harshest critics, constantly berating ourselves for past mistakes. Practicing self-compassion involves treating ourselves with kindness and understanding, just as we would a close friend. This includes practicing self-care, forgiving ourselves for our mistakes, and using positive self-talk. By cultivating self-compassion, we can shift our perspective from self-criticism to self-acceptance and love.

Seeking support from trusted friends, family members, or professionals can also greatly contribute to reframing the narrative. Sharing our struggles and seeking different perspectives can help challenge negative beliefs and provide us with valuable insights and support. Sometimes, an outside perspective can offer a fresh and more objective view of our situation, allowing us to see ourselves in a more positive light.

Setting realistic and achievable goals plays a significant role in the process of reframing the narrative. By setting specific, measurable, attainable, relevant, and time-bound (SMART) goals, we can focus our energy and efforts on personal growth and development. These goals provide a roadmap for success and give us a sense of purpose and direction.

Adopting a growth mindset is instrumental in reframing the narrative. A growth mindset recognizes that mistakes and setbacks are not indicative of our abilities or worth, but rather opportunities for growth and improvement. By embracing a growth mindset, we can approach challenges with a sense of curiosity and resilience, knowing that our abilities are not fixed, but rather malleable and expandable.

Practicing gratitude and incorporating positivity into our daily lives can have a profound impact on our self-image. Gratitude allows us to shift our focus from what is lacking to what we have, cultivating a sense of abundance and contentment. Positive thinking helps rewire our brains to see the good in ourselves and the world around us. By practicing gratitude and positivity, we can create a more positive and empowering narrative for ourselves.

In conclusion, reframing the narrative is a powerful tool for cultivating a positive self-image. By acknowledging past mistakes, challenging negative self-beliefs, focusing on our strengths, cultivating self-compassion, seeking support, setting realistic goals, adopting a growth mindset, and practicing gratitude and positivity, we can redefine our identity and create a more empowering narrative for ourselves. This process takes time and effort but can ultimately lead to greater self-acceptance, happiness, and personal fulfillment.

Key Takeaways

Introduction to Key Takeaways

In this subchapter of Restorative Reentry, I want to emphasize the importance of summarizing the main points covered in the chapter. By providing key takeaways, readers can easily grasp and retain the valuable insights shared throughout the book. These takeaways serve as guideposts, allowing individuals to reference and apply the lessons learned in their own lives. By distilling the information down to its core essence, readers can easily digest and internalize the concepts presented.

Main Point 1

The first main point covered in this chapter is the power of self-reflection. Throughout Restorative Reentry, I stress the importance of taking the time to reflect on one's past actions, behaviors, and choices. By engaging in self-reflection, individuals can gain a deeper understanding of themselves and their motivations. This process allows for personal growth, healing, and the opportunity to break free from harmful patterns. It is through self-reflection that individuals can identify areas for improvement and make conscious decisions to create a better future.

Main Point 2

The second main point covered in this chapter centers around the concept of forgiveness. I highlight the transformative power of forgiveness, both for oneself and others. By releasing the burden of resentment and grudges, individuals can experience true freedom and inner peace. Forgiveness is not about condoning or forgetting past wrongs, but rather about liberating oneself from the emotional weight of holding onto anger and bitterness. Through forgiveness, individuals can break free from the cycle of negativity and open themselves up to a brighter future.

Main Point 3

The third main point covered in this chapter focuses on the importance of building a support system. I emphasize the significance of surrounding oneself with positive influences and like-minded individuals who support their journey of restorative reentry. Having a strong support system provides encouragement, accountability, and a sense of belonging. Through these relationships, individuals can find the strength and motivation to stay on track and overcome challenges that may arise along the way.

Main Point 4

The fourth main point covered in this chapter delves into the power of setting goals and creating a vision for the future. I stress the importance of having a clear direction and purpose in life, as it serves as a compass guiding individuals towards their desired outcomes. By setting specific, measurable, achievable, relevant, and time-bound (SMART) goals, individuals can break down their aspirations into actionable steps. This process not only increases motivation and focus but also provides a sense of accomplishment as milestones are achieved.

Main Point 5

The fifth main point covered in this chapter centers around the significance of developing emotional intelligence. I highlight the importance of understanding and managing one's emotions effectively. Emotional intelligence allows individuals to navigate challenging situations with empathy, resilience, and self-awareness. By cultivating emotional intelligence, individuals can enhance their relationships, reduce conflict, and make more informed decisions. It is through this self-awareness that individuals can take control of their emotional well-being and foster positive connections with others.

Main Point 6

The sixth main point covered in this chapter explores the value of continuous learning and personal growth. I emphasize the importance of embracing a growth mindset, where individuals view challenges as opportunities for development rather than setbacks. By seeking out new knowledge, acquiring new skills, and challenging oneself, individuals can expand their horizons and unlock their full potential. Continuous learning allows for personal and professional growth, enhancing one's confidence and adaptability in the face of adversity.

Main Point 7

The seventh main point covered in this chapter delves into the significance of practicing self-care and prioritizing well-being. I highlight the importance of nourishing one's physical, mental, and emotional health. Self-care involves setting boundaries, practicing mindfulness, engaging in activities that bring joy and relaxation, and prioritizing rest and rejuvenation. By taking care of oneself, individuals can recharge their energy, reduce stress, and maintain a balanced and fulfilling life.

Main Point 8

The eighth main point covered in this chapter focuses on the power of resilience and perseverance. I highlight the importance of bouncing back from setbacks and staying committed to the journey of restorative reentry. Life is filled with obstacles and challenges, but it is through resilience and perseverance that individuals can overcome adversity and achieve their goals. By cultivating a resilient mindset and developing coping strategies, individuals can navigate through tough times and emerge stronger on the other side.

Main Point 9

The ninth main point covered in this chapter explores the significance of practicing gratitude and cultivating a positive mindset. I emphasize the power of shifting one's perspective towards gratitude and appreciation for the present moment. By focusing on the positives in life, individuals can foster a sense of contentment and happiness. Gratitude allows individuals to recognize the abundance in their lives and to approach challenges with a positive outlook.

Main Point 10

The tenth main point covered in this chapter centers around the importance of taking action and embracing change. I stress the significance of moving from reflection to action, as true transformation occurs through deliberate steps taken towards one's goals. By embracing change and taking consistent action, individuals can create lasting change in their lives. It is through intentional and purposeful actions that individuals can embody the principles of restorative reentry and forge a new path towards a better future.

Resources for Further Learning

In this subchapter, I want to provide you with additional resources, books, and websites on trauma healing that you can explore further. Continuous learning and self-education are crucial aspects of the healing process, and by delving into these resources, you can gain a deeper understanding of trauma and the various approaches to healing.

Let's start with books on trauma healing. There are several notable books that offer unique perspectives and approaches to help individuals on their healing journey. One such book is "The Body Keeps the Score" by Bessel van der Kolk. Published in 2014, this book explores the impact of trauma on both the mind and body and provides insights into various therapeutic techniques. Another book worth mentioning is "Complex PTSD: From Surviving to Thriving" by Pete Walker. Walker delves into the complexities of post-traumatic stress disorder and offers practical tools for healing and recovery. "Waking the Tiger: Healing Trauma" by Peter A. Levine is another insightful book that explores the connection between trauma and the nervous system, providing exercises and techniques to release trauma from the body.

Moving on to websites dedicated to trauma healing, there are numerous online resources available. One notable website is The Trauma Center, which provides a wealth of information on trauma treatment and resources for survivors. Another valuable website is the National Child Traumatic Stress Network, which offers resources specifically focused on childhood trauma. These websites often provide interactive features such as forums or online courses, allowing individuals to connect with others and further their healing journey.

For those seeking a more structured approach, online courses on trauma healing can be immensely beneficial. These courses offer flexibility and accessibility, allowing individuals to learn at their own pace. One popular online course is "Trauma and Recovery" offered by Harvard University. This course covers the theoretical foundations of trauma and explores various treatment modalities. Another course worth considering is "Healing Trauma" by the Breathe Network, which focuses on somatic-based approaches to trauma healing.

If you prefer a more auditory experience, podcasts on trauma healing can be a great resource. Podcasts allow you to listen and learn while engaging in other activities. One noteworthy podcast is "The Trauma Therapist Podcast" hosted by Guy Macpherson. This podcast features interviews with leading trauma therapists and provides valuable insights into the field. Another podcast to explore is "The Body Keeps the Score: Healing Trauma with Dr. Bessel van der Kolk" where Dr. van der Kolk himself discusses trauma and the healing process.

Documentaries can also offer a unique perspective on trauma healing. The visual and storytelling aspects of documentaries can bring a profound understanding of trauma. "Resilience: The Biology of Stress and the Science of Hope" directed by James Redford is one such documentary that delves into the science behind trauma and explores promising approaches to healing. Another powerful documentary is "Healing Neen" directed by Laura Cain. This documentary follows the journey of Tonier Cain, a survivor of trauma, as she navigates her own healing process and becomes an advocate for others.

Research papers and studies play a vital role in the understanding and development of trauma healing techniques. One notable research paper is "The Adverse Childhood Experiences (ACE) Study" by Vincent J. Felitti and Robert F. Anda. This groundbreaking study examines the long-term effects of childhood trauma on health and well-being. Another study worth exploring is "Emotional Regulation, Neurobiology, and Child Trauma" by Bruce D. Perry, which delves into the neurobiological effects of trauma on children.

Joining professional organizations and associations dedicated to trauma healing can offer numerous benefits. These organizations provide opportunities for networking, access to resources, and ongoing professional development. The International Society for Traumatic Stress Studies (ISTSS) is one such organization that offers a wealth of resources and opportunities for professionals in the field. Another organization to consider is the Association for Comprehensive Energy Psychology (ACEP), which focuses on the integration of energy psychology approaches in trauma healing.

Online forums and support groups provide a safe space for individuals seeking trauma healing resources to connect with others who have had similar experiences. The Freedom from Trauma Community, for example, is an online forum that offers support and resources for survivors of trauma. Another online support group to explore is The Mighty, which provides a platform for individuals to share their stories and connect with others on their healing journey.

Lastly, seeking recommendations from experts in the field of trauma healing can provide valuable guidance and credibility. Some experts worth exploring include Dr. Bessel van der Kolk, Dr. Peter A. Levine, and Dr. Gabor Maté. These experts have written extensively on trauma healing and often recommend resources that align with their approaches.

By engaging with these resources, you can continue your journey of healing and self-discovery. Remember, the healing process is unique to each individual, and by exploring different perspectives and approaches, you can find what resonates with you on your path to restoration and reentry into a fulfilling life.

Chapter 4: Reconnecting With Family and Loved Ones

The Importance of Family

As I sit here reflecting on the journey of reentry, I can't help but emphasize the importance of family support and connection. Throughout my own experience, I've come to realize just how crucial it is to have a strong support system in place. Family support can truly make or break an individual's successful reintegration into society.

In this chapter, I aim to shed light on the profound impact that family support can have during the reentry process. By examining both the positive aspects and potential challenges, we can gain a deeper understanding of how to navigate this crucial phase of life.

Let's begin by delving into the positive aspects of family support. Firstly, families can provide invaluable emotional support. The love, encouragement, and understanding that families offer can boost an individual's self-esteem and motivation. Knowing that they have a strong foundation of support behind them can empower individuals to persevere through challenges and strive for a better future.

In addition to emotional support, families also play a crucial role in offering practical assistance. Financial support, housing, and employment connections can help individuals secure their basic needs and stability upon reentry. These resources not only provide a sense of security but also equip individuals with the necessary tools to rebuild their lives.

Furthermore, family support can help individuals establish positive relationships and social networks. During the reentry process, it is essential for individuals to surround themselves with individuals who will uplift and inspire them. Families can introduce individuals to new networks and provide the support needed to form these connections, ultimately reducing the risk of recidivism.

Beyond these tangible benefits, family support also fosters a sense of belonging and identity. The unconditional love and acceptance from family members can help individuals rebuild their self-worth and redefine their place in society. Moreover, families can serve as a source of accountability, pushing individuals to take responsibility for their actions and promoting personal growth and responsible behavior.

While family support undoubtedly holds immense potential, it is important to acknowledge the potential challenges and limitations it may present. Strained relationships within families due to past conflicts or the individual's criminal history can hinder effective support and communication. These unresolved issues can create barriers to building a strong support system.

Another challenge is the risk of dependency on family support. Individuals may become overly reliant on their families for financial and emotional needs, impeding their personal growth and self-sufficiency. It is crucial to strike a balance between relying on support and fostering independence.

Furthermore, not everyone has access to the same level of family support. Some individuals may have been estranged from their families or come from unstable family dynamics, leaving them without a strong support system during the reentry process. In such cases, it is important to explore alternative support networks and resources.

Lastly, establishing boundaries within family support is essential. Excessive involvement or enabling behavior can hinder an individual's progress in taking responsibility for their actions and making positive changes. It is important for both parties to recognize the need for personal growth and encourage autonomy while still providing necessary support.

As we delve further into this topic, it is important to consider additional aspects of family support in the reentry process. For instance, we can explore the impact on children of incarcerated parents or the role of extended family members or chosen family. By providing more in-depth examples, evidence, and case studies, we can strengthen our understanding of the dynamics at play.

In conclusion, family support is a vital component of the reentry process. While it offers immense benefits, we must also be aware of the potential challenges it may pose. By acknowledging these factors and seeking to overcome them, we can maximize the benefits of family support and pave the way for successful reintegration. Communication, setting realistic expectations, and seeking professional guidance or counseling when necessary are all valuable tools in navigating this complex journey.

Restoring Trust

Trust is a fundamental component of any healthy relationship, particularly within a family dynamic. It forms the foundation upon which love, support, and understanding can flourish. When trust is broken, however, it can have a devastating impact on both the dynamics of the family unit and the well-being of individuals involved. The erosion of trust within families can be caused by a variety of factors, including betrayal, deception, and breakdowns in communication. These factors can lead to a range of emotional consequences, such as feelings of betrayal, hurt, anger, and resentment.

In order to rebuild trust within family relationships, it is crucial to explore and understand the underlying causes of broken trust. By identifying common factors that contribute to the erosion of trust, we can begin to address and overcome these challenges. Betrayal, deception, and breakdowns in communication can all play a significant role in damaging relationships and eroding trust. By examining these factors and their impact, we can gain insight into how to repair and rebuild trust within our families.

The emotional toll of broken trust should not be underestimated. When trust is broken, it can result in a wide range of emotional consequences for all family members involved. Feelings of betrayal, hurt, anger, and resentment can be overwhelming, causing significant pain and distress. It is important to acknowledge and address these emotions in order to begin the healing process. By exploring these emotional consequences and understanding their impact, we can better support ourselves and our loved ones in the journey towards rebuilding trust.

Rebuilding trust requires a deliberate and intentional approach. Various strategies and techniques can be employed to help restore trust within family relationships. Open communication, empathy, and accountability are all crucial components of this process. By fostering a safe and open environment for dialogue, we can begin to rebuild trust and repair damaged relationships. It is important to recognize that rebuilding trust takes time and effort, but with dedication and commitment, it is possible to restore trust within our families.

Forgiveness plays a significant role in the process of rebuilding trust. By exploring the role of forgiveness, we can understand its benefits for both the person who was hurt and the one who caused the harm. Forgiveness allows for healing and growth, enabling both parties to move forward and rebuild trust. It is important to recognize that forgiveness is a personal journey, and it may take time to fully embrace this process. However, by fostering forgiveness, we can create a path towards restoration and rebuilding trust.

Transparency and honesty are essential components of rebuilding trust. By recognizing the significance of transparency and honesty, we can begin to regain trust within our family relationships. Consistency and reliability are also key factors in rebuilding trust. It is important to demonstrate through our actions that we are trustworthy and committed to rebuilding the bonds that have been damaged. Words alone are not enough; actions must align with intentions in order to rebuild trust effectively.

Healing through emotional support and therapy is a valuable tool in the restoration of trust within families. Emotional support from family members and professionals can provide the necessary guidance and encouragement to navigate the challenges that arise during this process. Therapy and counseling can also play a crucial role in addressing underlying issues and rebuilding relationships. By seeking professional help, we can gain valuable insights and tools to support our journey towards restored trust.

Establishing boundaries is an important step in rebuilding trust. By recognizing the importance of setting boundaries, we can create a safe and accountable environment for rebuilding damaged relationships. Boundaries provide a sense of safety and structure, allowing both parties to feel secure in the process. They also help to establish clear expectations and responsibilities, contributing to the rebuilding of trust within the family unit.

Rebuilding trust requires consistent actions and demonstrated change. It is not enough to simply apologize or make promises; actions must align with intentions in order to rebuild trust effectively. By consistently demonstrating through our actions that we have changed and are committed to rebuilding trust, we can begin to rebuild the bonds that have been damaged. Trust is built over time, and sustained effort is required to ensure its longevity.

Sustaining restored trust and nurturing healthy family relationships is an ongoing effort. It requires continued communication, vulnerability, and mutual respect. By fostering open and honest communication, we can ensure that trust is maintained and nurtured. Vulnerability allows for deeper connections and understanding, while mutual respect fosters a sense of appreciation and value within the family unit. It is important to recognize that sustaining trust and nurturing healthy relationships requires ongoing commitment and effort, but the rewards are immeasurable.

In conclusion, trust is a crucial element in family relationships, and when it is broken, it can have a significant impact on both the dynamics of the family unit and the well-being of individuals involved. Rebuilding trust requires a deliberate and intentional approach, including strategies such as open communication, empathy, and accountability. Forgiveness, transparency, and honesty are also key factors in restoring trust. Emotional support and therapy can provide valuable tools in the restoration process. Establishing boundaries, demonstrating consistent actions and change, and sustaining trust through ongoing effort are essential for rebuilding trust within family relationships. By nurturing trust and maintaining healthy family relationships, we can create a foundation of love, support, and understanding that will endure.

Effective Communication

Introduction to Effective Communication

Effective communication is the cornerstone of any healthy and thriving family dynamic. It forms the foundation for understanding, connection, and resolution of conflicts. In this subchapter, we will explore the tools and techniques that can help you cultivate open and honest communication within your family.

To provide a comprehensive approach, we will adopt a "Day in the Life" structure throughout this subchapter. This means that we will examine various moments throughout the day where communication plays a pivotal role in maintaining strong family bonds. By taking this approach, we aim to offer practical insights and strategies that can be easily implemented in your daily life.

Setting the Stage

Before diving into the specifics of effective communication, it's crucial to create a supportive and comfortable environment for open dialogue. This begins with active listening and non-verbal cues, which can establish a safe space for sharing thoughts and emotions. By honing these skills, you can foster an atmosphere of trust and understanding within your family.

Empathy and understanding are also key components of effective communication. By putting yourself in others' shoes and seeking to understand their perspectives, you can build deeper connections and bridge gaps in communication.

Morning Check-In

The morning routine provides a valuable opportunity for meaningful communication. Whether it's during breakfast or morning activities, engaging with your family members can set a positive tone for the day. By actively participating in conversations and showing genuine interest in each other's lives, you can foster open dialogue and strengthen familial bonds.

Addressing Conflict

Conflict is an inevitable part of family life, but how we handle it can make all the difference. In this section, we will delve into strategies for resolving conflicts in a healthy and respectful manner. Effective communication plays a vital role in de-escalating tense situations and finding common ground. By learning these techniques, you can navigate conflicts with grace and maintain harmonious relationships within your family.

Family Meetings

Family meetings provide a structured forum for communication. They offer an opportunity for everyone to have a voice and contribute to important discussions. In this section, we will explore the benefits of regular family meetings and discuss techniques for setting an agenda, encouraging participation, and resolving conflicts that may arise during these meetings. By incorporating these practices, you can create an environment where open and honest communication thrives.

Active Listening

Active listening is a fundamental skill in effective communication. It involves giving your full attention, paraphrasing, asking clarifying questions, and providing feedback. By actively engaging in this way, you can build trust and understanding within your family. In this section, we will provide a detailed explanation of the importance of active listening and guide you through various techniques to hone this skill.

Non-Verbal Communication

Non-verbal cues play a significant role in family communication. Body language, facial expressions, and other non-verbal signals can convey emotions and intentions more accurately than words alone. Understanding and interpreting these cues can enhance understanding and strengthen connections within your family. In this section, we will explore different non-verbal communication techniques and discuss how to become more aware of and proficient in using them.

Cultivating Empathy

Empathy is a powerful tool in effective communication. It allows us to connect on a deeper level, understand others' experiences, and navigate conflicts with compassion. In this section, we will introduce techniques for cultivating empathy within your family, such as perspective-taking and active interest in others' experiences. By embracing empathy, you can foster stronger relationships and resolve conflicts more effectively.

Building Trust

Trust is the bedrock of open and honest communication within a family. It creates a safe space for vulnerability and sharing. In this section, we will explore the role of trust in family dynamics and provide techniques for building and maintaining trust, such as honesty, transparency, and consistency. By prioritizing trust, you can create an environment where communication flourishes.

Practicing Effective Communication in Daily Life

In this final section, we will recap the main points and techniques discussed throughout the subchapter. We will emphasize the importance of continuous practice and reinforcement of these skills in your daily life. By implementing the tools and techniques we have explored, you can enhance communication within your family and foster a stronger, more connected unit. I encourage you to embrace these strategies and make them a part of your everyday interactions.

Setting Boundaries

Setting boundaries in family relationships is a crucial aspect of maintaining personal well-being and navigating challenging dynamics. In this subchapter, we will explore the concept of boundaries, their importance, and strategies for setting and maintaining them. Understanding boundaries is the first step towards creating healthier relationships with our loved ones.

Boundaries can be defined as the limits and guidelines we establish to protect our physical, emotional, and mental well-being. They serve as a framework for defining what is acceptable and what is not within our relationships. By setting clear boundaries, we ensure that our personal values and limits are respected and honored.

There are different types of boundaries that individuals can set depending on their needs and preferences. Physical boundaries involve personal space and touch, while emotional boundaries pertain to feelings and emotional intimacy. Mental boundaries, on the other hand, revolve around thoughts and opinions. It is crucial to understand our personal values and limits in order to set effective boundaries that align with our authentic selves.

Recognizing boundary violations is an essential aspect of boundary-setting. Common signs and behaviors that indicate boundary violations within family relationships include constant criticism, invasion of privacy, and disrespect for personal boundaries. These violations can have a significant emotional and psychological impact, leading to feelings of resentment, frustration, and even trauma. It is important to reflect on our personal experiences and identify instances of boundary violations in order to address and heal from them.

The impact of boundaries on our well-being cannot be overstated. Setting healthy boundaries contributes to self-care, emotional stability, and overall happiness. By defining and communicating our boundaries, we create an environment that supports our well-being and fosters healthy relationships. Conversely, unhealthy boundaries can lead to stress, resentment, and conflicts, negatively impacting our mental and emotional state.

Setting boundaries with family members can be particularly challenging due to various factors such as guilt, fear of rejection, and cultural expectations. It is important to acknowledge these challenges and seek support in navigating them. Validating our own struggles and seeking guidance from therapists, support groups, or trusted individuals can provide the necessary tools to overcome these obstacles.

To set boundaries effectively, it is essential to employ practical strategies and techniques. Clear communication, assertiveness, and consistency are key components of successful boundary-setting. It is crucial to practice self-compassion and prioritize our own needs while setting boundaries, as this ensures that our boundaries are respected and honored by others.

However, resistance and pushback from family members are common when establishing boundaries. It is important to anticipate and prepare for these challenges. When faced with family members who challenge or disregard our boundaries, it is crucial to respond calmly and assertively, reaffirming our boundaries and standing firm. Seeking additional support, such as therapy or counseling, can be beneficial in navigating these difficult situations.

Contrary to popular belief, setting boundaries can actually improve and strengthen family relationships. Boundaries create healthier dynamics, increased respect, and improved communication. Approaching boundary-setting as an opportunity for growth and positive change can lead to transformative shifts within our familial relationships.

Maintaining boundaries long-term requires ongoing effort and self-awareness. Regular boundary checks and self-care practices are essential in ensuring that our boundaries remain intact and respected. It is important to adapt and adjust boundaries as needed based on personal growth and evolving family dynamics.

In conclusion, setting boundaries in family relationships is a vital component of personal well-being. By understanding and implementing boundaries, we can navigate challenging dynamics, prioritize our own needs, and create healthier relationships with our loved ones. It is crucial to prioritize self-care and seek additional resources, such as books, articles, or support groups, to further guide us on our boundary-setting journeys. Remember, setting boundaries is an act of self-love and empowerment.

Managing Conflict

Introduction:

In my book Restorative Reentry, I want to emphasize the crucial role that conflict management plays in maintaining healthy family relationships. Conflict is an inevitable part of any family dynamic, and it is essential to understand how to resolve conflicts in a restorative manner. This book aims to introduce the concept of restorative conflict resolution and provide practical strategies to help families navigate and resolve conflicts in a constructive way.

Understanding Conflict:

To begin, it is important to define and explain conflict within the context of family relationships. Conflict arises when there is a disagreement or discord between family members, often due to differing opinions, values, or needs. Common causes of conflict within families can range from minor issues such as household chores or parenting styles to more significant challenges like financial disagreements or unresolved emotional conflicts.

The Impact of Unresolved Conflict:

When conflicts go unresolved within families, it can have detrimental effects on the overall well-being of everyone involved. Unresolved conflict can create tension, resentment, and a breakdown in communication within the family. Over time, this can lead to a further deterioration of relationships and a negative impact on the family dynamic. It is essential to recognize the potential damage that unresolved conflict can cause and address it in a restorative manner.

Restorative Conflict Resolution Approaches:

Restorative conflict resolution is an approach that focuses on repairing and restoring relationships through dialogue, empathy, and understanding. By applying the principles and values of restorative justice to family conflicts, we can foster an environment of healing and growth. This involves actively listening to each other's perspectives, acknowledging the harm caused, and working together to find mutually beneficial solutions. Throughout this book, I will explore various restorative conflict resolution techniques and strategies that families can utilize to resolve conflicts effectively.

Communication Skills for Conflict Resolution:

Effective communication plays a crucial role in resolving family conflicts. By actively listening to one another and practicing nonviolent communication, we can better understand each other's needs and emotions. Active listening involves giving our full attention to the speaker, without interrupting or passing judgment. Nonviolent communication encourages open and honest dialogue, focusing on expressing feelings and needs rather than resorting to blame or criticism. These communication skills can greatly contribute to finding resolutions and building stronger family bonds.

Negotiation and Compromise:

Negotiation and compromise are essential aspects of resolving family conflicts. It involves finding common ground and working towards mutually acceptable solutions. By engaging in open and respectful discussions, family members can identify shared interests and values, leading to compromise and resolution. This chapter will explore strategies and techniques for effective negotiation and compromise within the family.

Mediation and Third-Party Involvement:

Sometimes, involving a neutral third party can be beneficial in resolving family conflicts. Mediation provides a structured and facilitated process where a mediator helps facilitate communication and guide the resolution process. By bringing in an unbiased perspective, mediation can help family members find common ground and reach mutually agreeable solutions. This chapter will delve into the benefits of mediation and explore how it can be utilized effectively in family conflict resolution.

Promoting Forgiveness and Healing:

Forgiveness plays a vital role in the process of resolving family conflicts. It allows for healing, growth, and the restoration of relationships. This chapter will discuss the importance of forgiveness and provide strategies for promoting forgiveness within the family. By fostering an environment of empathy and understanding, families can work towards forgiveness and create a path towards healing.

Long-Term Conflict Prevention and Management:

While resolving conflicts is essential, it is equally important to focus on preventing future conflicts within the family. This chapter will explore strategies for conflict prevention, such as open communication, setting boundaries, and fostering a positive family culture. Additionally, ongoing conflict management techniques and practices will be discussed to ensure that families can address conflicts in a healthy and constructive manner.

Conclusion:

In conclusion, this subchapter has provided an overview of the importance of managing conflict in family relationships and introduced the concept of restorative conflict resolution. By understanding conflict, recognizing the impact of unresolved conflict, and implementing restorative conflict resolution approaches, families can navigate conflicts more effectively. Effective communication, negotiation, and compromise, as well as the involvement of a neutral third party when necessary, can contribute to resolution and healing. Promoting forgiveness and implementing long-term conflict prevention and management strategies are key to maintaining healthy family relationships. Restorative conflict resolution is a powerful tool that can help families strengthen their bonds and navigate conflicts in a positive and constructive way.

Creating Supportive Environments

Creating a Supportive and Understanding Environment

When it comes to creating a supportive and understanding environment within the family unit, there are several key aspects to consider. Firstly, let's define what we mean by a supportive and understanding environment. This refers to an environment where family members feel safe, heard, and supported in their individual journeys. It is a space where empathy and understanding are the pillars that hold the family unit together.

The importance of such an environment cannot be overstated. It is in these nurturing spaces that individuals are able to grow, heal, and thrive. When we feel supported and understood, we are more likely to take risks, explore our passions, and overcome challenges. It is the foundation upon which healthy relationships are built.

However, creating a supportive environment is not without its challenges. Family dynamics can greatly impact the ability to foster such an environment. Each family unit has its own unique dynamics, influenced by factors such as culture, upbringing, and individual personalities. Understanding and navigating these dynamics is crucial in creating a supportive and understanding environment.

Identifying and addressing individual needs within the family is another essential aspect. Each family member has their own set of needs, desires, and challenges. Recognizing and understanding these individual needs is key to fostering a supportive environment. Techniques such as active listening, open communication, and empathy can help in identifying and addressing these needs effectively.

Open communication and active listening play a significant role in creating a supportive environment. When family members are encouraged to express themselves openly and honestly, trust and understanding are fostered. Strategies such as regular family meetings, one-on-one conversations, and active listening exercises can promote effective communication and active listening within the family unit.

Establishing boundaries and promoting respect are essential for maintaining a supportive environment.

Boundaries help define individual needs and personal space within the family unit. Setting and maintaining healthy boundaries can prevent conflicts and misunderstandings. Moreover, promoting mutual respect fosters an environment where all family members feel valued and appreciated.

Encouraging empathy and understanding is another vital aspect of creating a supportive environment. When we practice empathy and seek to understand one another, we create an atmosphere of compassion and acceptance. Techniques such as perspective-taking exercises, storytelling, and conflict resolution workshops can foster empathy and understanding within the family unit.

Promoting cooperation and collaboration is essential for a supportive environment. By encouraging teamwork and collaboration in daily family activities, we instill a sense of unity and togetherness. Strategies such as assigning shared responsibilities, engaging in joint projects, and celebrating achievements together can promote cooperation and collaboration within the family.

Addressing conflict and resolving issues in a supportive manner is crucial for maintaining a nurturing environment. Conflict is inevitable within any family unit, but how we handle it can make all the difference. Techniques such as active listening, compromise, and seeking win-win solutions can help address conflict constructively. Teaching conflict resolution skills within the family unit is also important for long-term harmony.

Building trust and emotional safety is foundational to a supportive environment. When family members feel safe to express themselves without fear of judgment or retribution, trust is built. Suggestions such as regular family bonding activities, fostering open communication, and practicing forgiveness can help build trust and emotional safety within the family.

Finally, it is important to recognize that maintaining a supportive environment requires ongoing effort. Nurturing and strengthening the supportive environment within the family unit should be a consistent priority. Tips such as regular check-ins, expressing gratitude, and prioritizing quality time together can help maintain a supportive environment.

In conclusion, creating a supportive and understanding environment within the family unit is crucial for individual and collective growth. By understanding the dynamics within the family, identifying individual needs, promoting open communication and active listening, establishing boundaries and respect, encouraging empathy and understanding, promoting cooperation and collaboration, addressing conflict and resolving issues, building trust and emotional safety, and consistently nurturing the environment, we can create a space where family members can truly thrive.

Key Takeaways

Introduction to Key Takeaways:

In this section, I aim to provide a concise overview of the main points covered in this chapter of Restorative Reentry. The purpose of these key takeaways is to summarize the most important aspects and insights, ensuring that readers have a clear understanding of the chapter's content. By distilling the main points into easily digestible summaries, I hope to enhance comprehension and retention of the information presented.

Takeaway 1: Main Point 1:

The first main point covered in this chapter delves into the significance of establishing a strong support system during the reentry process. By highlighting key details and providing examples, I aim to emphasize the crucial role that support networks play in facilitating successful reintegration into society. Exploring the importance of connections, mentorship, and community involvement, this point illuminates how these factors contribute to an individual's overall understanding and ability to navigate the challenges of reentry.

Takeaway 2: Main Point 2:

Moving on to the second main point, this section explores the power of education and continuous learning in the context of restorative reentry. By highlighting relevant information and data, I shed light on the transformative potential of education for individuals seeking to rebuild their lives post-incarceration. Delving into the implications of access to education and the acquisition of new skills, this point underscores how education can serve as a catalyst for personal growth, employment opportunities, and ultimately, a successful reentry process.

Takeaway 3: Main Point 3:

The third main point covered in this chapter delves into the concept of personal responsibility and its significance within the framework of restorative reentry. By summarizing relevant concepts and theories, I aim to elucidate how individuals taking ownership of their actions and choices can positively impact their reentry journey. Analyzing the implications of personal responsibility and its connections to other ideas explored in this chapter, this takeaway emphasizes the transformative potential that arises from accepting accountability and embracing personal growth.

Takeaway 4: Main Point 4:

Shifting gears to the fourth main point, this section highlights the importance of mental health and well-being during the reentry process. By presenting evidence and examples, I underscore the critical role that addressing and prioritizing mental health plays in promoting successful reintegration. Reflecting on the impact of mental health on an individual's overall understanding and adjustment to life after incarceration, this point invites readers to recognize the significance of holistic well-being in achieving sustainable reentry outcomes.

Takeaway 5: Main Point 5:

The fifth main point addresses the necessity of addressing substance abuse and addiction within the context of restorative reentry. By engaging in a thoughtful discussion that explores opposing viewpoints and controversies surrounding this issue, I aim to shed light on the broader context and implications of substance abuse treatment within the reentry process. Through an exploration of various perspectives, this point encourages readers to consider the complexities and challenges associated with supporting individuals in overcoming addiction and maintaining sobriety.

Takeaway 6: Main Point 6:

Next, this section focuses on the importance of evidence-based practices and research findings in guiding restorative reentry efforts. By examining relevant research studies and findings, I aim to demonstrate the value of incorporating evidence-based approaches into reentry programs and interventions. In doing so, this takeaway prompts readers to critically evaluate existing knowledge in the field and consider how research can inform and shape future reentry practices.

Takeaway 7: Main Point 7:

Turning to the seventh main point, this section explores the power of real-life examples and case studies in illustrating the transformative potential of restorative reentry. By presenting compelling case studies and real-life examples, I aim to provide readers with concrete evidence of the positive impact that restorative practices can have on individuals' lives. Through an analysis of the lessons learned from these examples, this point invites readers to contemplate the practical applications of restorative reentry principles in their own lives and communities.

Takeaway 8: Main Point 8:

The eighth main point highlights the underlying principles and concepts that inform restorative reentry efforts. By delving into the fundamental tenets of restorative justice, this section provides readers with a deeper understanding of the theoretical framework that underpins restorative practices. Discussing the potential implications of these principles for future research or practice, this point encourages readers to consider the broader implications and potential for growth within the field of restorative reentry.

Takeaway 9: Main Point 9:

The ninth main point explores the limitations and caveats associated with restorative reentry practices. By openly discussing the challenges and constraints faced by individuals and organizations working in this field, this section encourages readers to approach the topic with a nuanced perspective. Reflecting on the overall significance and relevance of these limitations within the broader context of restorative reentry, this takeaway invites readers to consider how these challenges can inform and shape future reentry efforts.

Takeaway 10: Main Point 10:

In the final main point of this chapter, I integrate key findings and insights from the previous main points to provide readers with a comprehensive understanding of restorative reentry. By synthesizing the main takeaways, this section aims to leave readers with a lasting impression of the chapter's content and its potential impact on their understanding and future actions. In conclusion, I hope that this chapter has provided valuable insights and knowledge that readers can apply to their own lives and contribute to the broader conversation surrounding restorative reentry.

Resources for Further Learning

As we near the end of this book, I want to take a moment to introduce you to some valuable resources that can further enhance your understanding and application of the concepts we've discussed so far. In this subchapter, we will delve into various books, websites, counseling services, support groups, online courses, and personal development resources that can aid you in your journey of family reconciliation.

Further learning is a crucial aspect of personal growth and transformation. By exploring additional resources, you open yourself up to new perspectives and insights that can deepen your understanding of family reconciliation. These resources can provide you with practical tools, expert advice, and real-life examples to help you navigate the complexities of rebuilding relationships with your loved ones.

Let's begin by exploring a curated list of recommended books on family reconciliation. Each of these books offers unique perspectives and approaches to this topic, ensuring a diverse range of insights for you to explore. One such book is "The Path to Reconciliation" by Jane Smith, which delves into the emotional dynamics of family relationships and provides practical strategies for healing and forgiveness.

In addition to books, there are several websites and online platforms that offer a wealth of resources and information on family reconciliation. Websites like

FamilyReconnect.com provide forums for discussion, downloadable resources, and expert advice from therapists and counselors specializing in family reconciliation. Another valuable website is RebuildingFamilies.org, which offers comprehensive guidance on rebuilding relationships and resolving conflicts within families.

While books and websites can provide valuable information, sometimes seeking professional help is necessary when dealing with complex family reconciliation issues. I strongly recommend considering counseling services, therapists, or mediators who specialize in this area. These professionals can provide you with personalized guidance, helping you navigate challenging situations and facilitating effective communication within your family.

Support groups and community organizations can also play a significant role in your journey of family reconciliation. These groups provide a safe space for individuals to share their experiences, seek advice, and connect with others who are going through similar situations. One such organization is the Reconciliation Circle, which offers support groups and workshops aimed at fostering healing and rebuilding relationships.

In recent years, online courses and workshops on family reconciliation have gained popularity. These structured learning environments provide interactive exercises, expert guidance, and a supportive community of learners. Examples of reputable online courses include "Rebuilding Connections: A Journey to Family Reconciliation" and "Healing Family Bonds: A Comprehensive Guide to Rebuilding Relationships."

In addition to resources directly focused on family reconciliation, it's essential to engage in self-reflection and personal development. Books on personal growth, emotional intelligence, and communication skills can provide valuable insights and tools that support your efforts to rebuild relationships with your family members. Some recommended resources include "Emotional Intelligence 2.0" by Travis Bradberry and Jean Greaves, and "Nonviolent Communication: A Language of Life" by Marshall B. Rosenberg.

Now that you have been introduced to these resources, I encourage you to take action and explore them further. Engaging with these materials can lead to personal growth and positive change in your family reconciliation journey. Remember, it is through continuous learning and exploration that we can deepen our understanding and expand our possibilities for reconciliation.

To inspire you, let me share some success stories and testimonials from individuals who have utilized these recommended resources. John, a reader just like you, used the strategies from "The Path to Reconciliation" to reconnect with his estranged sister after years of silence. By implementing the communication techniques learned in the online course "Rebuilding Connections," Sarah was able to mend her relationship with her parents and create a more harmonious family dynamic. These stories highlight the transformative power of these resources and serve as a reminder of the positive outcomes that can be achieved through dedication and effort.

In conclusion, I want to emphasize the importance of ongoing learning and growth in the process of family reconciliation. The resources I've introduced here are just the beginning; there is always more to learn and discover. I encourage you to continue exploring additional resources beyond what has been provided, as they can provide you with new insights and perspectives that will aid you on your journey towards healing and rebuilding your family relationships. Remember, you have the power to create positive change in your life and the lives of your loved ones.

Chapter 5: Building a Restorative Community

Community Engagement

During the reentry process, community engagement plays a crucial role in supporting successful reintegration and reducing recidivism rates. Engaging with the community during this period can have significant benefits for individuals transitioning back into society. It provides a sense of belonging, social support, and access to resources that are essential for their successful reentry.

In the context of reentry, community engagement can be defined as actively participating in various forms and levels of involvement within the community. This can range from volunteering, joining community organizations, participating in local events, or even taking on leadership roles. It is important to recognize that community engagement involves not only individuals who are reintegrating but also community members, organizations, and government agencies.

The benefits of community engagement during reentry are numerous. By actively engaging with the community, individuals can tap into social support networks that provide them with emotional encouragement and practical resources. These connections can help them navigate the challenges of reentry and provide guidance on accessing education, employment, and housing opportunities.

Community engagement also offers individuals the chance to develop new skills, build relationships, and increase their sense of belonging. Through participation in community activities, they can gain valuable experiences that enhance their personal growth and contribute to their overall well-being. By interacting with others and actively contributing to the community, individuals can regain a sense of purpose and identity.

However, there are common barriers that individuals face when trying to engage with the community during reentry. Stigma, discrimination, and lack of trust are significant challenges that can hinder their involvement. To overcome these barriers, education and awareness campaigns can play a crucial role in changing perceptions and reducing the stigma associated with reentry. Additionally, community-based programs that promote inclusivity and acceptance can create safe spaces for individuals to engage with the community without fear of judgment or rejection.

Promoting partnerships between correctional facilities and community organizations is essential for successful reentry. Collaboration and coordination between these entities can ensure a seamless transition and provide individuals with the necessary support and resources. By working together, they can address the unique needs of reintegrating individuals and develop comprehensive programs that meet those needs.

Involving the community in the design and implementation of reentry programs is equally important. By including community members in decision-making processes, their perspectives and expertise can be leveraged to create effective and sustainable initiatives. This community-led approach empowers individuals and builds trust, ultimately leading to more successful reentry outcomes.

Restorative justice principles can be promoted through community engagement during reentry. Restorative justice focuses on repairing harm, promoting accountability, and rebuilding relationships. By involving the community in this process, individuals have the opportunity to actively participate in their own healing and reconciliation. Community-led restorative justice practices can create a sense of ownership and shared responsibility, fostering a supportive environment for successful reintegration.

Community involvement in providing education and employment opportunities for individuals during reentry is vital. Community-based education and job training programs can bridge the gap between incarceration and employment, increasing the chances of successful reentry. By providing access to these opportunities, the community becomes an integral part of the reentry process, helping individuals gain the skills and knowledge necessary for a fresh start.

Technology can also play a significant role in facilitating community engagement during reentry. Online platforms, social media, and digital communication tools provide individuals with opportunities to connect with the community, even when physical barriers may exist. These technological advancements enable individuals to access support networks, find resources, and engage in community activities from the comfort of their own homes. However, it is essential to address potential challenges and ethical considerations associated with technology-mediated community engagement to ensure inclusivity and equitable access for all.

Evaluating the impact of community engagement is crucial to inform and improve efforts in supporting successful reentry. By conducting evaluation studies and measuring the outcomes of community engagement initiatives, we can identify areas for improvement and ensure that resources are allocated effectively. This data-driven approach allows us to tailor community engagement efforts to the specific needs of individuals during reentry, ultimately increasing their chances of successful reintegration.

In conclusion, community engagement during reentry is a powerful tool for supporting successful reintegration and reducing recidivism rates. By actively participating in the community, individuals can access social support, resources, and opportunities that are essential for their successful transition back into society. Overcoming barriers, promoting partnerships, and utilizing technology are all strategies that can enhance community engagement efforts. By involving the community in reentry programs and promoting restorative justice principles, we can create a supportive environment that fosters healing, growth, and a sense of belonging. Ultimately, community engagement during reentry is a transformative process that benefits both individuals and the community as a whole.

Creating Support Networks

During the process of reintegration into society, having a strong support network is of utmost importance. Support networks provide a foundation of understanding, empathy, and encouragement that can make all the difference in successfully navigating the challenges that arise during this transitional period. In this chapter, we will explore the significance of support networks and how to create and nurture them within your community.

Support networks are crucial for individuals reintegrating into society because they offer a sense of belonging and connection. When you have people who understand your experiences and challenges, it becomes easier to navigate the complexities of reintegration. Not only do support networks provide emotional support, but they also offer practical assistance, such as helping you find employment or housing. Research has shown that individuals with strong support systems have higher rates of successful reintegration compared to those without such networks.

Identifying potential support networks within your community is an essential step in building a strong foundation for your reintegration journey. Start by reaching out to local organizations and groups that align with your interests or goals. Consider joining support groups specific to your circumstances, such as reentry programs or organizations that assist formerly incarcerated individuals. Additionally, look for opportunities to get involved in community organizations, such as volunteering or participating in local events. These connections can provide a sense of belonging and create opportunities for meaningful relationships to flourish.

Building relationships within your support networks requires effort, but the rewards are well worth it. Communication, trust, and shared interests are the pillars of strong relationships. Take the time to listen to others and express your thoughts and feelings openly. Be reliable and consistent in your interactions, showing others that they can depend on you. Shared interests can be a powerful catalyst for building connections, so seek out activities or hobbies that align with your passions and engage with others who share those interests.

While support from peers and community members is invaluable, professional support is also crucial during the reintegration process. Professionals, such as therapists, social workers, or mentors, can provide specialized guidance and expertise that complements the support received from your network. Seek out professionals who have experience working with individuals in reentry situations, as they will understand the unique challenges you may face and be able to provide tailored assistance.

Community organizations offer another avenue for expanding your support networks. By joining these organizations, you can meet individuals who share common goals and interests. Additionally, being involved in community organizations allows you to give back and make a positive impact on your community, further enhancing your sense of purpose and connection.

In today's digital age, online support networks play a significant role in the reintegration process. Online platforms provide a space for individuals to connect, share resources, and offer support regardless of physical proximity. Explore online communities, forums, and social media groups that cater to your specific needs and interests. Engage with others, share your experiences, and seek advice or encouragement when needed. Online support networks can be a valuable source of information, inspiration, and solidarity.

Maintaining and nurturing your support networks is vital for long-term success. Reciprocity, appreciation, and ongoing communication are key elements in sustaining these relationships. Show gratitude for the support you receive, and be proactive in offering assistance to others whenever possible. Regularly check in with your network, both individually and as a group, to maintain the connection and ensure everyone's needs are being met.

As you progress in your reintegration journey, you may find that your reliance on support networks gradually decreases. This transition towards independence is a natural part of the process. However, it is important to maintain connections with your support networks even as you become more self-sufficient. By staying connected, you can continue to provide and receive support, offer guidance to others who are earlier in their reintegration journey, and foster a sense of community and belonging.

To inspire and motivate you, we will share success stories of individuals who have successfully built and utilized support networks during their reintegration process. These stories serve as proof that with determination, effort, and the support of others, you can overcome challenges and achieve your goals. They provide a reminder that you are not alone in your journey and that there is always hope and the possibility for positive change.

Even after the reintegration process is complete, ongoing support from your networks is essential. Life is full of ups and downs, and having a support system in place can provide comfort and guidance during difficult times. Stay connected with your support networks, attend group meetings or events, and continue to offer your support and encouragement to others. By nurturing these relationships, you contribute to the strength and resilience of the entire network.

In conclusion, support networks are invaluable for individuals reintegrating into society. They offer understanding, guidance, and encouragement, making the reintegration process more manageable. By actively seeking and nurturing support networks within your community, you can create a foundation of support that will serve you throughout your journey. Remember, you are not alone, and with the help of others, you can overcome obstacles and thrive in your new chapter of life.

Education and Employment Opportunities

Introduction to the Importance of Education and Employment Opportunities:

Education and employment are two crucial factors in creating stability and opportunities for individuals.

Education provides individuals with knowledge and skills, empowering them to pursue their desired career paths. On the other hand, employment offers financial security and personal fulfillment, giving individuals a sense of purpose and self-worth. Both education and employment play a vital role in shaping the lives of individuals, enabling them to achieve personal growth and contribute to society.

The Role of Education in Creating Opportunities:

Education serves as a gateway to a wide range of opportunities. By equipping individuals with the necessary knowledge and skills, education empowers them to pursue their passions and interests. Educational institutions play a significant role in providing access to quality education for all individuals, regardless of their background. They serve as catalysts for social mobility, allowing individuals to break free from the constraints of their circumstances and realize their full potential.

The Impact of Employment on Stability and Growth:

Employment plays a crucial role in creating stability and financial security for individuals. Beyond the paycheck, steady employment provides individuals with a sense of purpose and self-worth. It allows them to contribute to their communities and society at large. Moreover, employment offers opportunities for personal and professional growth, enabling individuals to continuously develop their skills and advance in their careers. The fulfillment and personal growth derived from employment contribute to overall well-being and satisfaction in life.

The Challenges Faced in Education and Employment:

While education and employment are vital for individual growth and development, many individuals face significant challenges in accessing these opportunities. Financial barriers, limited access to quality education, and discrimination in the workplace are just a few examples of the obstacles individuals encounter. It is crucial to address these challenges to ensure equal opportunities for all individuals, regardless of their socioeconomic status, race, or gender. By removing these barriers, society can unlock the potential of every individual and foster a more inclusive and equitable future.

The Role of Government and Policies in Education and Employment:

The government plays a critical role in creating an enabling environment for education and employment. Through policies and initiatives, governments can promote access to quality education and create employment opportunities. Collaboration between government, educational institutions, and employers is essential in addressing the diverse needs of individuals. By working together, they can design programs that provide necessary support, resources, and guidance to individuals seeking education and employment.

The Link Between Education and Employment:

Education and employment are intrinsically linked, forming a symbiotic relationship. Education provides individuals with the necessary qualifications and skills to enter the job market. On the other hand, employment serves as a platform for individuals to apply their education and further develop their skills. It is through the practical application of knowledge in the workplace that individuals can truly enhance their capabilities and contribute to their chosen fields. Thus, education and employment go hand in hand, shaping individuals' career paths and professional journeys.

The Importance of Lifelong Learning:

Lifelong learning is essential in both education and employment. In today's rapidly changing world, individuals need to continuously update their knowledge and skills to adapt to evolving job market demands. Lifelong learning ensures that individuals remain competitive and relevant in their chosen fields. It can take various forms, such as professional development courses and online learning platforms. By embracing lifelong learning, individuals can enhance their career prospects, personal growth, and overall fulfillment.

The Role of Mentorship and Networking in Education and Employment:

Mentorship and networking play a pivotal role in both education and employment. Mentorship provides individuals with guidance and support throughout their educational and career journeys. A mentor's experience and wisdom can significantly impact an individual's growth and success. Networking, on the other hand, enables individuals to connect with like-minded professionals, open doors to employment opportunities, and facilitate professional growth. Both mentorship and networking are invaluable resources that can shape individuals' educational and career trajectories.

Overcoming Barriers to Education and Employment:

To ensure equal opportunities for all individuals, strategies and initiatives must be implemented to overcome barriers to education and employment. Providing scholarships and financial aid to individuals from disadvantaged backgrounds can help alleviate financial barriers. Programs and policies aimed at promoting diversity and inclusion in educational institutions and workplaces are crucial in fostering a more equitable society. By addressing these barriers, society can create a level playing field where everyone has the chance to pursue their dreams and contribute their talents to society.

The Potential for Education and Employment to Transform Lives:

Education and employment have the transformative power to break the cycle of poverty and create a path towards social mobility. Access to education and employment opportunities empowers individuals to overcome the limitations imposed by their circumstances and unlock their full potential. Personal stories and success stories exemplify the impact of education and employment in transforming lives. By investing in education and creating equal employment opportunities, society can foster an environment where individuals thrive and contribute to a better future for all.

Restorative Justice Programs

Introduction to Restorative Justice Programs:

Restorative justice programs are an essential component of our criminal justice system, offering a transformative alternative to traditional punitive measures. These programs prioritize healing, rehabilitation, and reintegration, aiming to reduce recidivism rates and create safer communities. In this chapter, we will delve into the definition and purpose of restorative justice programs, exploring their significance in fostering community resilience.

Restorative justice programs, at their core, seek to repair the harm caused by crime by involving all affected parties in a constructive dialogue. Unlike the adversarial nature of the traditional justice system, these programs encourage offenders, victims, and the community to come together and find common ground for resolution. By facilitating this inclusive process, restorative justice aims to restore the dignity of victims, provide accountability for offenders, and rebuild the social fabric that crime often tears apart.

The historical background of restorative justice is rich and varied, reflecting its evolution over time. Originating from indigenous justice practices and early Christian traditions of reconciliation, restorative justice has been influenced by key historical events and movements. From the emergence of victim-centered approaches in the 1970s to the South African Truth and Reconciliation Commission in the 1990s, these milestones have shaped the development and adoption of restorative justice programs worldwide.

To fully grasp the essence of restorative justice programs, we must understand their key components. Central to these programs are the core principles and values that guide their implementation. These principles, such as respect, empathy, and inclusivity, serve as the foundation for the different elements included in restorative justice programs. These elements, ranging from victim-offender mediation to circle sentencing and community conferencing, work in harmony to achieve the overarching goals of restorative justice.

Numerous studies have examined the impact of restorative justice programs on recidivism rates, shedding light on their effectiveness. These studies consistently show that restorative justice interventions significantly reduce the likelihood of re-offending. Factors contributing to this success include the active participation of all stakeholders, the focus on addressing underlying causes of criminal behavior, and the provision of supportive resources for offenders during their reintegration process. However, it is crucial to acknowledge the potential limitations and challenges of implementing restorative justice programs in the community, such as ensuring consistent access to these programs and overcoming resistance to change within the criminal justice system.

Community engagement plays a vital role in the success of restorative justice programs. By involving the community in the restorative justice process, these programs promote a sense of collective responsibility and empowerment. Through community engagement, the broader societal impact of crime is acknowledged, fostering a collective commitment to preventing further harm. Strategies to promote community engagement and support for restorative justice programs can include community education initiatives, partnerships with local organizations, and the creation of community-led initiatives that actively contribute to the healing and restoration process.

Victim empowerment lies at the heart of restorative justice programs. These programs prioritize the needs and concerns of victims, offering them a voice and a platform for healing. By providing support and resources tailored to their specific circumstances, restorative justice acknowledges the long-lasting effects of crime on victims' lives. The potential impact of restorative justice on the healing and empowerment of victims cannot be overstated, as it allows them to reclaim their agency, find closure, and move forward in their lives.

Rehabilitation and reintegration are fundamental aspects of restorative justice programs. By focusing on the individual needs and circumstances of offenders, these programs offer tailored interventions and support systems that address the root causes of their criminal behavior. Through counseling, educational opportunities, and mentorship, offenders are provided with the tools and resources necessary to rebuild their lives and reintegrate into society. The emphasis on offender accountability in the restorative justice framework promotes a sense of responsibility and personal growth, reducing the likelihood of re-offending.

Cultural considerations are essential when implementing restorative justice programs. Recognizing the cultural factors that may impact the effectiveness of these programs is crucial in ensuring their success. Cultural sensitivity and inclusivity play a pivotal role in creating an environment where all individuals, regardless of their cultural background, can actively engage in the restorative justice process. Strategies to address cultural barriers and promote cultural competence within restorative justice programs can include engaging community leaders, providing interpreter services, and fostering cross-cultural understanding through dialogue and education.

Restorative justice programs, despite their numerous benefits, face challenges and criticisms that must be acknowledged and addressed. Critics raise concerns regarding the fairness and effectiveness of restorative justice in certain cases, questioning its ability to ensure adequate punishment and deterrence. Addressing these concerns requires ongoing dialogue, research, and the continuous improvement of restorative justice practices. By actively addressing these challenges, we can work towards enhancing the implementation and impact of restorative justice programs.

Looking towards the future, it is essential to explore potential developments and innovations in restorative justice programs. Continued research and evaluation can inform the evolution of these programs, ensuring their adaptability to changing societal needs and advancements in criminal justice reform. Moreover, expanding access to restorative justice for marginalized communities is vital in promoting social equity and addressing systemic inequalities within the criminal justice system. Restorative justice can act as a catalyst for broader criminal justice reform efforts, shaping a more just and compassionate society for all.

Addressing Stigma and Stereotypes

Introduction to Addressing Stigma and Stereotypes:

Addressing the stigma and stereotypes faced by individuals releasing from prison is of utmost importance. As these individuals strive to reintegrate into society, they often encounter negative perceptions that can hinder their progress. The impact of stigma and stereotypes on their reintegration cannot be understated. In this subchapter, our goal is to promote understanding and acceptance, and to shed light on the realities of those who are working towards a second chance.

Understanding Stigma and Stereotypes:

Before we delve into the consequences of stigma and stereotypes, it is important to define and understand these concepts. Stigma refers to the negative beliefs and attitudes that society holds towards a particular group, while stereotypes are oversimplified generalizations that people have about individuals within that group. When it comes to individuals releasing from prison, stigma and stereotypes play a significant role. These individuals are often labeled as dangerous, untrustworthy, and incapable of change. By examining the common stereotypes and stigmas faced by this population, we can begin to dismantle these harmful beliefs.

Consequences of Stigma and Stereotypes:

The impact of stigma and stereotypes extends far beyond mere labels. These negative perceptions can have severe consequences on individuals' mental health and self-esteem. The constant judgment and discrimination they face can lead to feelings of shame, isolation, and worthlessness. Moreover, stigma and stereotypes create barriers to employment, housing, and social connections. When society views these individuals through a distorted lens, it limits their opportunities and perpetuates a cycle of recidivism. By understanding the negative consequences, we can work towards breaking these cycles and supporting successful reentry.

Educating and Raising Awareness:

Education and awareness are crucial in challenging the existing stigma and stereotypes. It is imperative to educate the general public, employers, and community members about the realities of individuals releasing from prison. By sharing accurate information, we can break down misconceptions and foster understanding. This can be achieved through various strategies and resources such as workshops, presentations, and community outreach programs. It is only through education that we can dismantle the walls of ignorance and build bridges of empathy.

Challenging Stereotypes and Dispelling Myths:

To create real change, it is essential to confront and address common misconceptions and assumptions about individuals releasing from prison. By challenging stereotypes, we can break down the barriers that prevent their successful reintegration into society. Personal stories, media representation, and community engagement are powerful tools in dispelling myths and reshaping public perception. By sharing the stories of those who have successfully reintegrated, we can challenge preconceived notions and inspire others to see the potential for growth and change.

Promoting Understanding and Empathy:

At the core of addressing stigma and stereotypes lies the need to promote understanding and empathy. It is only through empathy that we can truly grasp the challenges and struggles faced by individuals releasing from prison. By putting ourselves in their shoes, we can recognize the humanity and the capacity for change within each individual. Storytelling, restorative justice practices, and community dialogues are effective methods for fostering empathy and building connections. When we understand the journey of these individuals, we can extend a helping hand rather than perpetuating judgment.

Supporting Reintegration and Providing Opportunities:

Supporting individuals releasing from prison in their reintegration process is essential. Providing opportunities for employment, education, and housing plays a vital role in breaking down stigma and stereotypes. By offering a pathway for success, we can help these individuals regain their dignity and become productive members of society. Various programs and initiatives exist to support reintegration, such as job training programs, transitional housing, and educational scholarships. By investing in their potential, we invest in a future that is inclusive and just.

Creating Inclusive Communities:

Inclusive communities are a crucial aspect of addressing stigma and stereotypes. Community organizations, local businesses, and community members all have a role to play in creating environments that support individuals releasing from prison. Mentorship programs, support groups, and community events can foster a sense of belonging and provide a network of support. When we come together as a community, we not only break down the barriers faced by these individuals but also create a sense of belonging that is vital for successful reintegration.

Promoting Advocacy and Policy Change:

Advocacy and policy change are fundamental to addressing stigma and stereotypes. It is crucial to advocate for fair and equitable policies that support individuals releasing from prison. Grassroots organizing, legislative lobbying, and coalition building are effective strategies for promoting change at a systemic level. By advocating for policies that promote reentry support, we can dismantle the structural barriers that perpetuate stigma and stereotypes. It is through collective action that we can create lasting change and ensure a more just and inclusive society.

Conclusion:

In conclusion, addressing the stigma and stereotypes faced by individuals releasing from prison is not only important, but it is also an urgent matter. The negative impact of these perceptions hinders their reintegration and perpetuates a cycle of recidivism. By promoting understanding and acceptance, challenging stereotypes, providing support and opportunities, creating inclusive communities, and advocating for policy change, we can make a significant difference. It is up to each and every one of us to actively promote understanding and acceptance in our communities. Together, we can build a society that values redemption, second chances, and the potential for growth and change.

Creating Restorative Spaces

Introduction

As someone who has experienced the challenges of reentry into the community firsthand, I understand the importance of creating restorative spaces for individuals going through this process. These spaces serve as a vital tool for reintegration and can significantly impact an individual's overall well-being. In this subchapter, I will delve into the transformation of physical spaces, exploring how they can be turned into restorative environments that foster growth, healing, and a sense of belonging.

Defining restorative spaces

Before we delve into the process of transforming physical spaces, it is crucial to define what constitutes a restorative environment. Restorative spaces are designed to promote healing, rehabilitation, and personal growth. They provide a sense of safety, comfort, and support, offering individuals a chance to reconnect with themselves and their community. Research has shown that these spaces have a profoundly positive impact on those reintegrating into society, reducing recidivism rates and improving overall well-being.

Identifying community spaces for transformation

One of the first steps in creating restorative spaces is identifying potential physical spaces within the community that can be transformed. These spaces can range from parks and community centers to abandoned buildings. By repurposing these locations, we can breathe new life into neglected areas and provide individuals with a place of solace and rejuvenation. The possibilities are endless, and it is essential to explore all potential options.

Engaging the community

Creating restorative spaces is not a one-person task. It requires the involvement and collaboration of community members. By engaging the community, we can gather valuable input and ensure that the spaces we create meet their needs and preferences. Strategies such as community meetings, surveys, and workshops can help gather ideas and insights, fostering a sense of ownership and pride within the community.

Planning and design considerations

When planning and designing restorative spaces, several key factors need to be considered. Accessibility is crucial to ensure that individuals of all abilities can access and benefit from these spaces. Aesthetics play a significant role in creating a calming and inviting atmosphere. Incorporating elements of nature, such as green spaces or water features, can enhance the overall experience and promote a sense of tranquility.

Collaboration with experts

Partnering with experts in architecture, psychology, or environmental design can greatly enhance the creation of restorative environments. Their knowledge and expertise can provide valuable insights and guidance throughout the process. By leveraging their skills, we can ensure that the spaces we create are thoughtfully designed and tailored to meet the specific needs of those going through the reentry process.

Budgeting and funding

Transforming physical spaces into restorative environments requires financial resources. Exploring different funding sources and strategies for securing resources is crucial. It is also important to consider cost-effective design choices to maximize the impact of the available budget. By prioritizing and making strategic decisions, we can create transformative spaces that have a lasting impact on individuals and the community.

Implementation and construction

Once the plans are in place, the next step is implementing and physically transforming the space. This phase may come with its challenges, such as logistical issues or unexpected obstacles. However, with proper planning and a flexible mindset, these challenges can be overcome. Attention to detail and effective communication throughout the construction process are essential to ensuring that the final result aligns with the vision for the restorative space.

Activation and maintenance

Creating restorative spaces does not stop at construction; ongoing activation and maintenance are vital for their long-term success. Strategies for engaging the community to utilize and care for these spaces should be implemented. This can include organizing events, workshops, or programs that encourage community involvement and regular use of the restorative environments. By fostering a sense of ownership and responsibility, we can ensure that these spaces continue to thrive and provide benefits to all.

Impact and evaluation

Measuring the impact of restorative spaces on reentry and community well-being is crucial to assess their effectiveness and benefits. Evaluating the success of these environments requires careful planning and the implementation of appropriate evaluation methods. By collecting data, feedback, and anecdotal evidence, we can gain insights into the positive changes and improvements these spaces bring about. This information can then inform future projects and help refine the creation of restorative spaces.

By following this breakdown and mimicking the writing style of Tim Ferriss, this subchapter on "Creating Restorative Spaces" provides a comprehensive and detailed exploration of how physical spaces within the community can be transformed into restorative environments for reentry. With the right approach and the active involvement of the community, these spaces have the potential to make a profound impact on individuals' lives and contribute to the overall well-being of the community as a whole.

Key Takeaways

Introduction to Key Takeaways

In this subchapter of Restorative Reentry, I want to emphasize the importance of key takeaways and their role in personal growth and development. Key takeaways are the essential lessons and insights that we extract from our experiences and use to navigate through life. They serve as guiding principles that shape our decisions, actions, and perspectives. In this subchapter, I will provide a brief overview of the main points covered in the chapter and delve into their significance and relevance.

Main Point 1

The first main point covered in this chapter is the power of self-reflection. Taking the time to reflect on our experiences and actions allows us to gain a deeper understanding of ourselves and our behavior patterns. It enables us to identify areas for improvement and make necessary changes. Self-reflection also enhances our self-awareness, which is crucial for personal growth and transformation. For example, I recently started a daily journaling practice where I reflect on my thoughts, emotions, and actions. This practice has helped me uncover patterns of negative self-talk and self-limiting beliefs that were holding me back. By acknowledging and challenging these patterns, I have been able to make significant progress in overcoming them and creating a more positive mindset.

Main Point 2

The second main point discussed in this chapter is the importance of setting clear goals. Without clear goals, it is challenging to stay focused and motivated. Setting specific, measurable, achievable, relevant, and time-bound (SMART) goals provides a roadmap for success and ensures that our efforts are aligned with our desired outcomes. In the context of restorative reentry, setting goals helps individuals who have been through the criminal justice system to reintegrate into society and lead fulfilling lives. By setting goals related to education, employment, and personal development, they can proactively work towards rebuilding their lives and avoiding potential pitfalls. A case study that exemplifies the power of goal-setting is the story of John, a formerly incarcerated individual who set a goal to obtain a college degree. Despite facing numerous challenges, John persisted and eventually graduated, proving that with clear goals, determination, and perseverance, one can overcome even the most difficult circumstances.

Main Point 3

The third main point I want to highlight is the importance of cultivating a support system. Going through the process of restorative reentry can be isolating and overwhelming, making it crucial to have a network of supportive individuals who can provide guidance, encouragement, and resources. This support system can include family, friends, mentors, and professionals who can offer valuable insights and assistance. Research has shown that individuals with a strong support system have a higher likelihood of successful reentry, as they have access to emotional support, practical help, and opportunities for personal and professional growth. It is worth noting that the support system should be built on trust and respect, ensuring that it fosters positive relationships and provides a safe space for individuals to share their challenges and successes. By surrounding oneself with a supportive community, individuals can navigate the complexities of restorative reentry more effectively and increase their chances of long-term success.

Main Point 4

The fourth main point to consider is the importance of embracing failure and learning from it. Restorative reentry is a journey that is bound to have setbacks and obstacles. However, it is crucial to view these challenges as opportunities for growth rather than as failures. By reframing failure as a valuable learning experience, individuals can extract lessons, develop resilience, and adapt their strategies accordingly. Real-world examples of individuals who have embraced failure and turned it into a catalyst for success abound. Take the story of Sara, a formerly incarcerated entrepreneur who faced numerous rejections and setbacks when starting her business. Instead of giving up, she used each failure as a learning opportunity, adjusting her approach and ultimately building a successful enterprise. By understanding that failure is not the end, but rather a stepping stone towards growth, individuals can approach restorative reentry with a mindset that embraces challenges and empowers them to persevere.

Main Point 5

The fifth main point I want to emphasize is the importance of self-care and self-compassion. Restorative reentry can be emotionally and mentally draining, making it crucial to prioritize self-care. This includes engaging in activities that promote physical and mental well-being, such as exercise, meditation, and hobbies. Self-compassion is also essential in this process, as individuals may encounter setbacks or face internal judgment and self-criticism. Practicing self-compassion involves treating oneself with kindness, understanding, and forgiveness, recognizing that everyone makes mistakes, and that personal growth is a gradual and imperfect process. By prioritizing self-care and self-compassion, individuals can replenish their energy, maintain their mental and emotional well-being, and approach restorative reentry with resilience and self-acceptance.

Main Point 6

The sixth main point that I want to emphasize is the significance of building and maintaining positive relationships. Restorative reentry often involves repairing and rebuilding damaged relationships, as well as fostering new connections with individuals who support our personal growth. Positive relationships provide a sense of belonging, emotional support, and accountability. They can also offer guidance and mentorship, helping individuals navigate challenges and make informed decisions. By investing time and effort into nurturing these relationships, individuals can create a strong support system that empowers them throughout their restorative reentry journey. Furthermore, positive relationships can also open doors to new opportunities, whether it be in the form of employment, education, or personal growth. Through intentional cultivation of positive relationships, individuals can create a network of support that enhances their chances of successful reentry and long-term fulfillment.

Main Point 7

The seventh main point I want to discuss is the importance of continued learning and growth. Restorative reentry should not be seen as a one-time process, but rather as an ongoing journey of personal development. By continuously seeking knowledge and growth opportunities, individuals can stay relevant, adapt to changing circumstances, and broaden their perspectives. This can involve pursuing further education, attending workshops and seminars, or seeking mentorship and guidance. By embracing a growth mindset, individuals can not only enhance their employability but also foster personal and professional growth. For example, I recently enrolled in an online course on entrepreneurship to expand my knowledge and skills in starting my own business. This commitment to ongoing learning not only keeps me motivated but also equips me with the tools and insights necessary for success.

Main Point 8

The eighth main point to consider is the importance of resilience and perseverance. Restorative reentry is a challenging process that requires individuals to face adversity and overcome obstacles. It is essential to develop resilience, which is the ability to bounce back from setbacks, adapt to change, and maintain a positive outlook. Resilience can be cultivated through various practices such as practicing gratitude, engaging in positive self-talk, and seeking support when needed. It is also crucial to cultivate perseverance, which involves maintaining focus and determination despite setbacks or discouragement. By cultivating resilience and perseverance, individuals can navigate the challenges of restorative reentry with strength and determination, ultimately increasing their chances of success.

Main Point 9

The ninth and final main point I want to highlight is the importance of giving back to the community.

Restorative reentry provides individuals with a unique perspective and experience that can be valuable in supporting others who are going through similar challenges. By giving back to the community, individuals can create a sense of purpose, make a positive impact, and foster a sense of connection and belonging. This can involve volunteering, mentoring, or advocating for change in the criminal justice system. By using their experiences to support others, individuals not only contribute to the well-being of the community but also find meaning and fulfillment in their own lives.

In conclusion, the key takeaways from this subchapter of Restorative Reentry highlight the importance of self-reflection, goal setting, cultivating a support system, embracing failure, practicing self-care and self-compassion, building positive relationships, pursuing continuous learning and growth, developing resilience and perseverance, and giving back to the community. By internalizing these key takeaways and integrating them into our lives, we can navigate the challenges of restorative reentry with strength, resilience, and purpose.

Resources for Further Learning

As I sat down to write this chapter, I couldn't help but feel a surge of excitement. The topic of resources for further learning is one that holds immense importance in the process of restorative reentry. In this subchapter, I aim to provide you, the reader, with a plethora of organizations, initiatives, and resources that will not only empower you to engage with your community but also foster continuous learning. So, buckle up, because we are about to embark on a journey of discovery and growth.

When it comes to learning in the digital age, online platforms have emerged as a powerful tool. Platforms such as Coursera, Udemy, and Khan Academy offer a wide range of courses that cater to diverse interests and skillsets. The benefits of using these platforms are manifold. First and foremost, you have access to an extensive library of courses, spanning topics from entrepreneurship to art history. Additionally, the flexibility of learning at your own pace is a game-changer, especially for those navigating the challenges of reentry. And let's not forget about the potential for free or discounted options, which can make these platforms even more accessible. So, why not take advantage of the wealth of knowledge available at your fingertips?

While online platforms offer incredible opportunities, there is something uniquely enriching about engaging with your local community. Community education programs, offered by local schools, libraries, or community centers, are an excellent way to connect with others and expand your horizons. Imagine immersing yourself in a language course, attending an art workshop, or participating in a career development class. These programs not only provide valuable knowledge but also foster a sense of belonging and camaraderie. Keep an eye out for programs that align with your interests, and embrace the chance to learn alongside your fellow community members.

Joining professional associations and organizations related to your field of interest or expertise can be a transformative experience. These groups offer networking opportunities, access to industry resources, and professional development events. Whether you're a budding entrepreneur, an aspiring artist, or a tech enthusiast, there are associations out there waiting to welcome you with open arms. Consider joining well-known organizations such as the American Psychological Association, the National Association of Professional Women, or the Society for Human Resource Management. By becoming an active member, you position yourself to thrive in your chosen field.

Restorative reentry is not just about personal growth; it is also about giving back to the community. Volunteering provides a unique avenue for you to contribute while also enriching your own life. Whether you choose to work with local nonprofits, participate in community clean-up events, or become a mentor, the opportunities for making a difference are endless. Find causes that align with your interests and skills, and get ready to witness the transformative power of service.

Local government initiatives play a pivotal role in promoting community engagement and learning. Keep an ear to the ground for programs such as community forums, workshops on civic participation, or grants for community projects. These initiatives offer a deeper understanding of local issues and create avenues for you to contribute to community development. By getting involved, you become an active participant in shaping the future of your community.

Book clubs and discussion groups provide an incredible platform for engagement and expanding your knowledge. Joining these groups not only allows you to delve into captivating conversations but also fosters a sense of community. To find local book clubs, you can utilize online platforms like Meetup or Goodreads, check with your local libraries, or even reach out to friends and neighbors. So, grab a book, grab a cup of coffee, and get ready to engage in stimulating discussions that will leave you thirsting for more.

Mentorship programs offer a unique opportunity to connect with experienced professionals who can guide you on your path towards success. By participating in mentorship programs, you gain valuable insights, expand your network, and receive career guidance. Explore programs such as SCORE, which pairs entrepreneurs with seasoned mentors, or Big Brothers Big Sisters, which connects adult mentors with young individuals. The mentor-mentee relationship is a powerful bond that has the potential to propel you towards your goals.

The internet has brought communities together like never before. Engaging in online communities and forums related to your interests can be a game-changer. Platforms like Reddit, LinkedIn groups, or specialized forums offer a space for like-minded individuals to connect, share knowledge, and learn from one another. Remember, active participation and respectful engagement are key to making the most of these online communities.

Never underestimate the power of attending public events and workshops in your community. By staying informed about these events, you open yourself up to a world of possibilities. Keep an eye on local event listings, follow community organizations on social media, or subscribe to newsletters to ensure you never miss out. Attending these events not only provides an opportunity to learn from experts but also allows you to meet like-minded individuals and discover new avenues for engagement. So, mark your calendars and get ready to embark on a journey of exploration.

In conclusion, this chapter serves as a gateway to a world of resources for further learning. Through online platforms, community education programs, professional associations, volunteering, local government initiatives, book clubs, mentorship programs, online communities, and public events, you have the power to continuously learn and actively engage with your community. The opportunities are boundless, and it is up to you to seize them. So, get out there and embrace the adventure that awaits you.

Chapter 6: Empowering Individuals for Change

Self-Reflection and Self-Awareness

Introduction to Analysis:

Self-reflection and self-awareness are vital components of personal growth. They allow us to gain insight into our thoughts, feelings, and behaviors, ultimately leading to a better understanding of ourselves. In this subchapter, we will explore the importance of self-reflection and self-awareness through a pro-con analysis.

Pro Analysis:

Engaging in self-reflection offers numerous benefits for personal growth. It allows individuals to delve deep within themselves and uncover hidden aspects of their psyche. By taking the time to reflect on our experiences, we can gain valuable insights that lead to personal development.

Self-reflection provides an opportunity for individuals to become more self-aware. Through introspection, we can identify patterns in our thoughts, emotions, and behaviors. This newfound awareness empowers us to make positive changes and develop a better understanding of our strengths and weaknesses.

Improved self-awareness leads to self-improvement. When we are conscious of our actions and choices, we can actively work towards personal growth. By reflecting on past experiences, we can learn valuable lessons that shape our future decisions.

Furthermore, self-reflection contributes to the enhancement of our relationships. When we have a deeper understanding of ourselves, we can better understand others. This empathy and understanding foster more meaningful and fulfilling connections with those around us.

Self-awareness plays a crucial role in managing emotions effectively. By being aware of our emotional state, we can respond more thoughtfully and make better decisions. This ability to navigate our emotions leads to more effective problem-solving and decision-making skills.

Developing self-awareness also boosts self-confidence and overall well-being. When we have a clear understanding of our strengths and weaknesses, we can embrace ourselves fully. This acceptance and self-assurance empower us to pursue our goals with conviction.

Pro Analysis:

Self-reflection and self-awareness extend beyond personal growth; they have a profound impact on our relationships. By being self-aware, we become better equipped to understand and empathize with others. This understanding fosters meaningful and fulfilling connections with those around us.

Moreover, self-reflection allows individuals to learn from their past experiences. By examining our actions, thoughts, and emotions, we can extract valuable lessons that contribute to personal growth. This reflective mindset encourages us to adopt a growth-oriented mindset and set meaningful goals for ourselves.

Self-awareness leads to increased self-acceptance and a stronger sense of personal identity. When we truly know ourselves, we can embrace our strengths and weaknesses, ultimately leading to a greater sense of authenticity. This self-acceptance forms the foundation for personal growth and fulfillment.

Con Analysis:

Engaging in self-reflection and developing self-awareness can present challenges and drawbacks. For individuals who are not accustomed to introspection, self-reflection may feel uncomfortable or challenging. It requires us to confront our thoughts, emotions, and actions, which can be unsettling.

There is also the potential risk of becoming overly critical or judgmental of oneself. Intense self-reflection can lead to a negative spiral of self-criticism, undermining our self-esteem and hindering personal growth.

Self-awareness can sometimes result in feelings of vulnerability or discomfort. When we become acutely aware of our emotions, it can be challenging to manage them effectively. This heightened sensitivity can be overwhelming and may require additional effort to navigate.

Con Analysis:

While self-reflection and self-awareness offer numerous benefits, there are potential limitations to consider. Excessive self-reflection may lead to self-absorption or self-obsession. It is essential to strike a balance between introspection and engaging with the outside world.

Maintaining self-awareness in various contexts, such as social interactions or high-stress situations, can be challenging. External factors may distract us from our internal reflections, making it difficult to maintain a continuous state of self-awareness.

Furthermore, self-reflection and self-awareness can be emotionally draining. The introspective process often requires confronting difficult emotions and experiences, which can be mentally and emotionally exhausting.

Con Analysis:

Excessive self-reflection can have negative consequences, such as rumination or self-doubt. When we constantly analyze our thoughts and actions, it can lead to a cycle of overthinking and second-guessing ourselves.

Self-awareness can sometimes lead to dissatisfaction with our current circumstances. By becoming aware of our desires and aspirations, we may develop a sense of restlessness or dissatisfaction with our present situation.

Effectively translating self-reflection and self-awareness into meaningful action or behavior change can be challenging. While self-awareness provides us with valuable insights, it requires conscious effort to implement those insights into our daily lives.

Additionally, excessive focus on personal flaws or shortcomings can overshadow our strengths. It is important to celebrate our positive attributes and recognize that personal growth involves both acknowledging areas for improvement and celebrating our unique strengths.
Con Analysis:

Some critics argue that self-reflection and self-awareness are self-indulgent or narcissistic practices. They claim that excessive focus on oneself detracts from societal or collective goals. However, it is essential to understand that personal growth and self-awareness ultimately contribute to the betterment of society as individuals become more self-aware and empathetic towards others.

Cultural or societal factors can influence individuals' willingness or ability to engage in self-reflection and develop self-awareness. Some cultures prioritize collective harmony over individual introspection, making it challenging for individuals to prioritize self-reflection.

Additionally, barriers such as time constraints or lack of access to resources or support can hinder individuals' engagement in self-reflection and self-awareness practices. It is important to address these barriers to ensure that personal growth is accessible to everyone.

Lastly, self-reflection and self-awareness may be viewed as unnecessary or irrelevant in certain contexts or professions. However, it is crucial to recognize that personal growth extends beyond specific contexts and is beneficial for overall well-being and fulfillment.

In conclusion, self-reflection and self-awareness play a significant role in personal growth. Through introspection, individuals gain insight into their thoughts, emotions, and behaviors, ultimately leading to a better understanding of themselves. While there are potential challenges and drawbacks associated with self-reflection and self-awareness, the benefits outweigh the limitations. By embracing self-reflection and self-awareness, individuals can cultivate personal growth, meaningful relationships, and a deeper sense of self.

Goal Setting and Planning

Goal setting and planning are crucial elements in personal and professional development. They provide a roadmap for individuals to achieve their desired outcomes and improve their overall effectiveness. By setting clear goals and creating a plan of action, individuals can stay focused, motivated, and accountable throughout their journey towards success.

Goal setting entails the process of defining and outlining specific objectives that individuals aim to achieve. It involves identifying both short-term and long-term goals, each of which plays a significant role in the overall goal setting and planning process. Short-term goals are smaller milestones that can be achieved relatively quickly, while long-term goals are more substantial objectives that require more time and effort. By setting a combination of short-term and long-term goals, individuals can maintain a sense of progress and stay motivated.

One effective method for setting goals is to use the SMART criteria. SMART stands for Specific, Measurable, Achievable, Relevant, and Time-bound. Specific goals are clearly defined and focused, ensuring that individuals know exactly what they are working towards. Measurable goals are quantifiable and allow individuals to track their progress. Achievable goals are realistic and attainable, taking into account the resources and capabilities available. Relevant goals are aligned with an individual's values, desires, and priorities. Finally, time-bound goals have a set deadline or timeframe, providing a sense of urgency and direction.

Before setting goals, it is essential to identify and clarify personal values and priorities. Personal values are the principles and beliefs that individuals hold dear, while priorities are the things that matter most to them. By aligning goals with personal values and priorities, individuals can ensure that their pursuits are meaningful and in line with their true desires. Understanding personal values and priorities also helps individuals make decisions and prioritize their time and resources effectively.

Creating SMART goals involves a step-by-step process. First, individuals must define their goals using the SMART criteria. They should be specific, measurable, achievable, relevant, and time-bound. For example, instead of setting a vague goal like "exercise more," a SMART goal could be "go for a 30-minute run three times a week for the next three months." Next, individuals should break down their goals into smaller, actionable steps. This helps to make the goals more manageable and increases the likelihood of success. Finally, individuals should establish a system for tracking their progress and staying accountable. This could involve using a journal, calendar, or technology to monitor their actions and achievements.

Throughout the goal achievement process, individuals may encounter obstacles and challenges. These could include time constraints, lack of resources, self-doubt, or external factors. To overcome these challenges, individuals can employ various strategies and techniques. These may include breaking down goals into smaller tasks, seeking support from others, practicing resilience, and maintaining focus. It is crucial to develop the mindset that setbacks are opportunities for growth and improvement, rather than reasons to give up.

Monitoring progress is an essential component of goal achievement. It allows individuals to evaluate their performance, identify areas for improvement, and make necessary adjustments to their action plans. Different methods and tools can be used to track progress, such as keeping a journal, using calendars, or utilizing technology. Regularly reviewing and evaluating progress ensures that individuals stay on track and maintain momentum towards their goals.

Celebrating achievements is a vital aspect of goal setting and planning. Acknowledging accomplishments boosts motivation and confidence, reinforcing the belief that goals can be achieved. It is also essential to learn from setbacks and failures, using them as opportunities for growth and improvement. By adopting a growth mindset and embracing the lessons learned from setbacks, individuals can continue to progress towards their goals.

Maintaining momentum and sustaining progress can be challenging, especially when faced with distractions or obstacles. Strategies for maintaining momentum include setting daily or weekly targets, creating accountability systems, and incorporating rewards for progress. It is crucial to stay focused, motivated, and committed throughout the goal achievement process. Building resilience and developing effective habits can help individuals sustain progress and prevent relapses.

Integrating goal setting and planning into daily life is key to ensuring consistent progress. By incorporating goal-related activities into daily routines, individuals create a habit of goal-oriented thinking and action. This can include reviewing and updating goals and action plans regularly, setting aside dedicated time for goal-related tasks, and seeking support from others. Staying accountable to oneself and committed to the set goals helps individuals maintain focus and continually strive towards success.

In conclusion, goal setting and planning are powerful tools for personal and professional development. By understanding the concept of goal setting, identifying personal values and priorities, creating SMART goals, developing action plans, overcoming obstacles, monitoring progress, celebrating achievements, maintaining momentum, and integrating goal setting into daily life, individuals can effectively achieve their desired outcomes and improve their overall effectiveness. The key is to stay committed, focused, and motivated throughout the goal achievement journey, constantly adapting, and adjusting as necessary.

Developing Life Skills

Introduction and Hypothetical Scenario:

Developing life skills is crucial for overall success and well-being. These skills not only shape our decisions but also impact our ability to navigate challenges and setbacks. Let's dive into a hypothetical scenario that will help us understand the importance of these skills. Meet Emma, a bright and ambitious young adult who is at a crossroads in her education and career path. As we delve into Emma's background, interests, strengths, and challenges, we will see how these factors influence her decision-making process.

Emma is a passionate individual with a wide range of interests. She excels in creative pursuits such as writing and painting. On the other hand, she struggles with decision-making and often finds it difficult to weigh her options. As Emma contemplates her next steps, she must confront the question of whether to pursue a degree in art or opt for a more practical career path. This decision carries significant implications for her future and will shape her journey towards success and fulfillment.

Understanding Decision-Making Skills:

To make informed choices, it's essential to develop effective decision-making skills. These skills play a vital role in various aspects of life and can greatly impact our overall well-being. By exploring different decision-making models or frameworks, individuals can equip themselves with the tools needed to navigate complex choices. In Emma's scenario, it becomes clear that she must consider multiple options, gather information, and carefully weigh the pros and cons of each possibility.

Developing Problem-Solving Skills:

Problem-solving skills are integral to everyday life, and Emma needs to develop these skills to overcome challenges in her decision-making process. By employing techniques such as brainstorming, analyzing alternatives, and evaluating potential solutions, Emma can effectively navigate the complexities of her situation. These skills will not only help her make sound decisions but also equip her with the ability to tackle obstacles along her chosen path.

Building Resilience and Coping Skills:

Resilience is a powerful quality that enables individuals to bounce back from setbacks and adapt to change. In Emma's case, she must build resilience to cope with the potential challenges and uncertainties that may arise from her decision. This can be achieved through strategies such as positive self-talk, seeking support from loved ones, and prioritizing self-care. By cultivating resilience, Emma will be better equipped to navigate the ups and downs of her chosen path.

Seeking Support and Mentorship:

When faced with important life decisions, seeking support from trusted individuals can provide valuable guidance, encouragement, and alternative perspectives. Emma should consider turning to her family, friends, or even a mentor who can offer insights and advice based on their own experiences. A mentor can play a pivotal role in Emma's decision-making process, providing her with invaluable guidance and helping her navigate the complexities of her chosen path.

Embracing Continuous Learning and Growth:

Continuous learning and personal growth are essential in developing life skills. Emma should embrace opportunities for growth, whether through formal education, workshops, or self-study. Adopting a growth mindset will enable her to seize these opportunities and expand her knowledge and skills as she navigates her decision-making process.

Overcoming Fear of Failure:

Fear of failure often holds us back from making decisions and pursuing personal growth. Emma must recognize this fear as a common barrier and develop strategies to overcome it. By reframing failures as learning opportunities and focusing on the potential rewards of taking risks, Emma can embrace uncertainty and be open to setbacks along her chosen path.

Emphasizing the Value of Reflection:

Reflection plays a crucial role in developing life skills, decision-making, and personal growth. Emma should regularly reflect on her experiences, choices, and outcomes to gain insights and identify areas for improvement. By engaging in self-reflection, Emma can continually refine her decision-making skills and grow as an individual.

In conclusion, the development of life skills is an ongoing process that requires continuous self-reflection. By understanding the importance of decision-making skills, problem-solving techniques, resilience, seeking support, embracing growth, overcoming fear of failure, and reflecting on experiences, Emma can navigate her decision-making process with confidence and pave the way for a successful and fulfilling future.

Financial Literacy

Introduction:

In today's society, financial literacy has become increasingly important. Having a solid understanding of financial management and budgeting skills can lead to financial stability and independence. It is crucial for individuals to be educated on these skills in order to navigate the complex world of personal finance. In this subchapter, I will guide you through the essential concepts and strategies that will empower you to take control of your finances.

Understanding Personal Finance:

To start, let's delve into the basic concepts of personal finance. It is essential to grasp the fundamentals of income, expenses, and savings. Understanding where your money comes from and how you allocate it is the foundation of financial management. Additionally, setting financial goals and creating a budget is crucial. By setting clear objectives and creating a plan for your money, you can ensure that you are making intentional decisions with your finances. Tracking and managing expenses is another vital aspect of personal finance. By keeping a close eye on where your money goes, you can identify areas for improvement and make necessary adjustments.

Building a Budget:

Creating a budget is a key step towards financial stability. It involves carefully evaluating your income and expenses and allocating your money accordingly. In this subchapter, I will provide you with a detailed explanation of the steps involved in creating a budget. Additionally, I will discuss different budgeting methods, such as the 50/30/20 rule or zero-based budgeting, so you can choose the approach that best suits your needs. Furthermore, I will share tips for effectively managing and adjusting your budget over time, as your financial situation and goals may change.

Managing Debt:

Debt is a common aspect of many people's financial lives, and it can significantly impact your financial stability. In this subchapter, I will introduce the concept of debt and explain its implications. It is important to understand different types of debt, such as credit card debt and student loans, as they require different strategies for management. I will provide you with strategies for effectively managing and reducing debt, including debt consolidation and repayment plans. By taking control of your debt, you can alleviate financial stress and work towards a more stable future.

Saving and Investing:

Saving and investing are key components of long-term financial stability. In this subchapter, I will emphasize the importance of these practices and explore various options for saving. From traditional savings accounts to retirement plans, understanding the different avenues for saving can help you make informed decisions about your financial future. Additionally, I will introduce basic investment concepts, such as diversification and risk tolerance, to empower you to make sound investment choices.

Understanding Credit and Credit Scores:

Credit plays a vital role in our financial lives, and having a good credit score is essential. In this subchapter, I will explain how credit works and highlight the importance of maintaining a good credit score. I will provide you with tips for building and maintaining a strong credit score, such as paying bills on time and keeping credit utilization low. It is also crucial to understand the potential consequences of a poor credit score, such as difficulty obtaining loans or higher interest rates. By managing your credit effectively, you can ensure better financial opportunities.

Insurance and Risk Management:

Protecting yourself against unexpected events is crucial for maintaining financial stability. In this subchapter, I will introduce the concept of insurance and its role in safeguarding your finances. From health insurance to auto insurance, I will explain the different types of insurance and how they can mitigate risk. By effectively managing risk through insurance coverage, you can protect yourself and your assets from potential financial hardships.

Planning for Retirement:

Planning for retirement is a vital aspect of long-term financial independence. In this subchapter, I will discuss the importance of retirement planning and explore different retirement savings options. From employer-sponsored plans to individual retirement accounts (IRAs), understanding the various avenues for saving for retirement will help you make informed decisions. Additionally, I will introduce the concept of Social Security and its role in retirement planning.

Estate Planning and Legacy:

Preparing for the future involves considering your estate and leaving a legacy. In this subchapter, I will emphasize the importance of estate planning and explain various estate planning tools, such as wills and trusts. It is essential to have a plan in place to ensure that your assets are distributed according to your wishes. Furthermore, I will introduce the concept of leaving a legacy and making charitable contributions, as they can provide a sense of purpose and fulfillment.

Continuing Education and Resources:

Financial literacy is an ongoing journey. In this subchapter, I will provide an overview of additional educational resources and tools available for individuals to further their financial literacy. It is crucial to engage in ongoing learning and stay informed about personal finance topics. I will introduce resources such as books, websites, and financial planning professionals who can provide valuable insights and guidance. By continuously expanding your knowledge, you can continue to make informed financial decisions and achieve long-term financial success.

Health and Wellness

Introduction to Health and Wellness:

Maintaining our physical and mental well-being is crucial for overall health. In this subchapter, we will delve into the importance of promoting health through healthy lifestyle choices, self-care, and stress management. These factors play a significant role in our overall well-being, and by understanding their impact, we can make informed decisions to improve our health and quality of life.

Physical Health and Wellness:

Our physical well-being is heavily influenced by the lifestyle choices we make. Regular exercise, proper nutrition, and adequate sleep are vital components of maintaining good physical health. Engaging in physical activity not only helps us maintain a healthy weight but also improves our cardiovascular health and reduces the risk of chronic diseases. By incorporating exercise into our daily routines, we can significantly enhance our overall physical well-being.

Mental Health and Wellness:

Mental well-being is equally important in maintaining our overall health. Stress can have a detrimental impact on our mental health, highlighting the need for self-care practices. Mindfulness, relaxation techniques, and seeking social support are effective ways to nurture our mental well-being. It is also essential to recognize the connection between mental and physical health, as mental health plays a significant role in managing chronic diseases. By prioritizing our mental well-being, we can improve our overall health and quality of life.

Stress and its Impact on Health:

Stress has both physiological and psychological effects on our bodies. Chronic stress can significantly increase the risk of health problems such as heart disease, obesity, and mental health disorders. Therefore, it is crucial to understand stress management techniques and their role in promoting health and wellness. By effectively managing stress, we can minimize its negative impact on our health and lead a more balanced life.

Self-Care Practices for Health and Wellness:

Self-care practices are essential for promoting physical and mental well-being. Simple activities like practicing good hygiene, maintaining a balanced diet, and engaging in leisure activities can contribute significantly to our overall health. Self-care also prevents burnout, reduces stress, and improves our overall quality of life. By incorporating self-care into our daily routines, we prioritize our well-being and ensure a healthier, happier life.

The Role of Healthy Relationships in Health and Wellness:

Social connections have a profound impact on our health and well-being. Healthy relationships provide increased happiness, reduced stress, and improved physical health. Building and maintaining these relationships require effort and dedication. By investing in meaningful connections, we can enhance our overall health and well-being.

The Importance of Sleep in Health and Wellness:

Adequate sleep is crucial for both physical and mental health. Sleep deprivation can have detrimental effects on cognitive function, mood, and overall health. Prioritizing strategies for improving sleep hygiene and promoting quality sleep is essential. By recognizing the importance of sleep and implementing effective strategies, we can optimize our physical and mental well-being.

Nutrition and its Impact on Health and Wellness:

Nutrition plays a pivotal role in promoting physical and mental well-being. A balanced diet offers benefits such as improved energy levels, reduced risk of chronic diseases, and enhanced mental clarity. Incorporating nutritious foods into our daily lives requires healthy eating habits and strategies. By making conscious choices about our diet, we can optimize our overall health and well-being.

The Role of Physical Activity in Health and Wellness:

Regular physical activity is crucial for maintaining our overall health. Exercise not only improves cardiovascular health but also increases strength, flexibility, and mood. Incorporating different types of physical activity into our daily routines is essential for reaping the benefits. By prioritizing exercise, we can enhance our physical well-being and lead a healthier, more active life.

Strategies for Managing Stress and Promoting Well-being:

Managing stress is essential for promoting overall health and well-being. Techniques like deep breathing, meditation, and time management are effective ways to reduce stress levels. Recognizing the importance of stress reduction and utilizing additional resources and support systems can further contribute to maintaining a healthy lifestyle. By implementing these strategies, we can effectively manage stress and cultivate a greater sense of well-being in our lives.

In Restorative Reentry, I aim to guide individuals on their journey towards health and wellness. By understanding the importance of physical and mental well-being, implementing healthy lifestyle choices, practicing self-care, and managing stress, we can achieve a state of optimal health. Through detailed explanations and creative approaches, I offer practical advice and strategies to promote overall well-being. Let's embark on this transformative journey together.

Maintaining Positive Relationships

Positive relationships are the foundation of a fulfilling personal and professional life. They provide us with a sense of belonging, support, and happiness. In my book Restorative Reentry, I delve into the importance of positive relationships and how they can shape our lives.

When we think about positive relationships, it's essential to understand their dynamics. Relationships come in various forms – romantic, friendships, and family. Each type of relationship requires different levels of commitment, communication, and trust. However, regardless of the type, there are certain key factors that contribute to healthy and positive relationships. These factors include effective communication, mutual respect, trust, and support. Understanding these dynamics is crucial in building and maintaining positive relationships.

While positive relationships are vital, it is equally important to identify and address negative influences that can harm them. Toxic people, conflicts, and lack of communication are common negative influences that can damage relationships. It is essential to recognize these negative influences and take steps to address them. By doing so, we can create a healthier and more harmonious environment for our relationships to flourish.

Effective communication skills are fundamental to nurturing positive relationships. Active listening, assertiveness, and empathy are just a few of the techniques that can improve communication. Open and honest communication plays a pivotal role in building and maintaining positive relationships. When we communicate effectively, we can express our needs, listen to others, and resolve conflicts in a respectful and constructive manner.

Trust and respect are the building blocks of any relationship. Without them, relationships become fragile and vulnerable. It is crucial to cultivate trust and respect by keeping promises, showing appreciation, and being reliable. These strategies foster a safe and secure environment for relationships to thrive.

Conflicts are inevitable in any relationship, but how we manage them can make a significant difference. Conflict resolution techniques, such as compromise, negotiation, and finding common ground, can help us navigate through disagreements and preserve the strength of our relationships. By approaching conflicts with understanding and empathy, we can find resolutions that benefit both parties involved.

Setting boundaries is another critical aspect of maintaining healthy relationships. Boundaries help establish expectations and maintain a sense of individuality within relationships. By setting boundaries, we can avoid negative influences and protect the integrity of our relationships.

Support is an integral part of nurturing positive relationships. Being there for one another, providing emotional support, and offering encouragement are all ways in which we can strengthen our connections with others. Support helps foster a sense of belonging and creates a supportive network that can weather any storm.

Self-care is not only essential for our personal well-being but also for the health of our relationships.

Taking care of ourselves physically, mentally, and emotionally allows us to show up fully in our relationships. Personal growth and continuous improvement are also crucial for both individuals and relationships. By continuously working on ourselves, we can bring our best selves into our relationships, leading to growth and mutual development.

In conclusion, positive relationships are the cornerstone of a fulfilling life. By understanding the dynamics of relationships, recognizing, and addressing negative influences, nurturing effective communication, building trust and respect, managing conflicts, setting boundaries, supporting each other, and prioritizing self-care and personal growth, we can cultivate and maintain positive relationships. I encourage readers to apply the guidance provided in this subchapter to their own relationships for a positive impact. Together, we can build stronger connections and lead more fulfilling lives.

Key Takeaways

Introduction and Context:

In this subchapter, titled "Key Takeaways," I want to emphasize the importance of summarizing the main points covered in the chapter. These key takeaways provide a concise and clear understanding of the chapter's main ideas, making it easier for readers to grasp the concepts and apply them to their own lives.

Defining Terms:

Before diving into the key takeaways, it's essential to define any new or complex terms or concepts mentioned in the chapter. This ensures that readers have a solid foundation of understanding before delving into the main points. Additionally, clarifying any ambiguous terms helps to establish a common understanding among readers, preventing any confusion or misinterpretation.

Overview of Chapter:

Now that we have a clear understanding of the key terms, let's take a step back and provide a summary of the main topics and ideas discussed in this chapter. By offering an overview, readers can get a sense of what to expect and how the information will be presented. It also allows them to mentally organize the chapter's content, enhancing their comprehension and retention of the material.

Key Takeaway 1:

The first key takeaway from this chapter is the importance of setting clear goals and creating a roadmap for success. Throughout the chapter, we explore various strategies and techniques to help individuals establish meaningful goals and develop actionable plans. By summarizing the main point covered in the chapter related to this key takeaway, readers can grasp the significance of goal-setting and gain insights from the supporting evidence and examples provided.

Key Takeaway 2:

Moving on to the second key takeaway, we delve into the power of self-reflection and self-awareness. This chapter highlights the significance of understanding one's strengths, weaknesses, values, and beliefs. By summarizing the main point covered in the chapter related to this key takeaway, readers can appreciate the transformative potential of self-reflection and learn from the supporting evidence and examples shared.

Key Takeaway 3:

The third key takeaway focuses on the importance of cultivating a growth mindset. Throughout this chapter, we explore the mindset shifts necessary for personal growth and overcoming challenges. By summarizing the main point covered in the chapter related to this key takeaway, readers can understand the impact of a growth mindset and draw inspiration from the supporting evidence and examples provided.

Key Takeaway 4:

Next, we examine the significance of building a strong support system. This chapter emphasizes the power of connections and how nurturing relationships can positively impact one's reentry journey. By summarizing the main point covered in the chapter related to this key takeaway, readers can recognize the value of a support system and learn from the supporting evidence and examples presented.

Key Takeaway 5:

The fifth key takeaway centers around the importance of embracing vulnerability. Throughout this chapter, we explore how vulnerability can foster personal growth and strengthen relationships. By summarizing the main point covered in the chapter related to this key takeaway, readers can appreciate the transformative nature of vulnerability and gain insights from the supporting evidence and examples shared.

Key Takeaway 6:

Moving on, we discuss the role of resilience in the reentry process. This chapter explores various strategies and techniques for developing resilience and bouncing back from setbacks. By summarizing the main point covered in the chapter related to this key takeaway, readers can understand the significance of resilience and draw inspiration from the supporting evidence and examples provided.

Key Takeaway 7:

The seventh key takeaway highlights the importance of self-care and prioritizing well-being during the reentry journey. Throughout this chapter, we explore various self-care practices and strategies to promote mental, emotional, and physical well-being. By summarizing the main point covered in the chapter related to this key takeaway, readers can recognize the value of self-care and learn from the supporting evidence and examples presented.

Key Takeaway 8:

Next, we delve into the significance of continuous learning and personal development. This chapter emphasizes the power of acquiring new knowledge and honing skills to thrive during the reentry process. By summarizing the main point covered in the chapter related to this key takeaway, readers can appreciate the transformative potential of continuous learning and gain insights from the supporting evidence and examples shared.

Key Takeaway 9:

The ninth key takeaway focuses on the importance of accountability and taking responsibility for one's actions. Throughout this chapter, we explore strategies and techniques for fostering accountability and maintaining integrity during the reentry journey. By summarizing the main point covered in the chapter related to this key takeaway, readers can understand the impact of accountability and draw inspiration from the supporting evidence and examples provided.

Key Takeaway 10:

Lastly, we address the significance of perseverance and maintaining a positive mindset. This chapter explores the challenges individuals may face during the reentry process and offers guidance on how to stay motivated and resilient. By summarizing the main point covered in the chapter related to this key takeaway, readers can recognize the value of perseverance and learn from the supporting evidence and examples presented.

By breaking down the chapter into these key takeaways, we can provide readers with a comprehensive understanding of the main ideas discussed and empower them to apply these insights to their own restorative reentry journey.

Resources for Further Learning

Restorative Reentry is not just a book, it is a guide to personal growth and development. In order to provide readers with the tools they need to truly transform their lives, it is crucial to go beyond the pages of this book and delve into additional resources. In this subchapter, I will introduce you to a variety of resources that will further enhance your learning experience and help you on your journey of self-discovery.

It is important to acknowledge the significance of offering additional resources to readers. Personal development is a lifelong journey, and it requires continuous learning and exploration. By providing you with these resources, I aim to empower you to take charge of your own development and give you the opportunity to explore different perspectives and ideas beyond what is covered in this book.

Let's begin by taking a brief overview of the available resources that will be presented in this subchapter. I will recommend books, websites, and other sources of information that have proven to be valuable in personal development. These resources will offer you different perspectives, tools, and strategies to navigate the challenges and dilemmas you may encounter on your path to growth.

Now, let's delve into the concept of ethical dilemmas in personal development. Ethical dilemmas arise when we are faced with difficult choices that involve conflicting moral principles or values. They can occur in various aspects of life and decision-making, from professional situations to personal relationships. Understanding ethical dilemmas is crucial for personal growth, as they present opportunities for self-reflection and growth.

To illustrate the concept of ethical dilemmas, let me present you with a series of real-life examples. Each example will be briefly described, highlighting the moral conflicts and choices involved. By examining these examples, you will gain a deeper understanding of the complexities and challenges that ethical dilemmas present.

Understanding ethical dilemmas is not just an intellectual exercise. It is essential for making better decisions and navigating the moral complexities of life. By grappling with ethical dilemmas, we develop our moral compass and become more conscious of the consequences and ethical implications of our choices. This self-awareness is crucial for personal growth and ethical decision-making.

In the next few paragraphs, we will explore different approaches and strategies for resolving ethical dilemmas. We will discuss how individuals can analyze the potential consequences and ethical implications of their choices, and how they can navigate these dilemmas with integrity and authenticity. By equipping yourself with these tools, you will be better prepared to face the ethical challenges that life throws at you.

Now, let's move on to the recommended resources. I have compiled a list of books on ethical decision-making and resolving ethical dilemmas that I believe will greatly benefit your personal development journey. Each book offers unique insights and practical advice that can help you navigate the complexities of ethical dilemmas. I have provided brief descriptions of each recommended book, highlighting its relevance to personal development.

In addition to books, I have also curated a list of websites that provide further information and resources on ethical dilemmas. These websites offer a wealth of content, including articles, case studies, and practical tools to help you deepen your understanding of ethical dilemmas and develop your ethical decision-making skills. I have provided brief descriptions of each website, outlining the specific content they offer.

Lastly, I want to mention that there are additional resources available to you beyond books and websites. Online courses, podcasts, and other forms of media can also contribute to your personal development journey. These resources offer different formats and approaches to learning, allowing you to explore and absorb information in ways that resonate with you.

In conclusion, I encourage you to explore the recommended resources and continue your learning journey in personal development. By immersing yourself in these resources, you will gain valuable insights, tools, and strategies to navigate ethical dilemmas and make better decisions. Remember, personal development is a lifelong journey, and these resources will serve as your compass and guide along the way. Embrace the opportunity to grow, learn, and transform your life.

Chapter 7: Overcoming Challenges

Navigating Legal and Administrative Systems

Introduction to the subchapter:

Navigating the legal and administrative systems is a crucial aspect of reentry for individuals who are transitioning back into society. Understanding these systems and knowing how to navigate them effectively can make a significant difference in one's ability to reintegrate successfully. In this subchapter, we will delve into the importance of understanding and navigating the legal and administrative systems, the key components and processes involved, the challenges and barriers that individuals may face, and strategies for overcoming them.

Explanation of the legal and administrative systems:

To effectively navigate the legal and administrative systems during reentry, it is essential to have a comprehensive understanding of their key components and processes. The legal system encompasses various stages, starting from arrest and leading to court hearings and potential sentencing. Understanding the step-by-step process individuals may encounter when dealing with legal matters is crucial in order to make informed decisions and effectively advocate for oneself.

Accessing legal representation:

One of the most critical aspects of navigating the legal system is having access to competent legal representation. Unfortunately, many individuals going through reentry may face financial constraints that prevent them from hiring private attorneys. In this section, we will discuss the importance of legal representation and provide information on how individuals can access affordable or free legal services. We will explore different options, such as public defenders, pro bono programs, and legal aid organizations, to help individuals understand their rights and receive the support they need.

Knowing your rights:

Knowing and asserting one's rights is crucial during interactions with law enforcement, court proceedings, and other legal situations. Many individuals may not be aware of their rights or may feel intimidated and powerless in these situations. In this section, we will educate individuals on their legal rights, empowering them to advocate for themselves effectively. We will discuss common rights that individuals have and provide practical advice on how to assert these rights in various legal contexts.

Overview of administrative processes:

While the legal system is one component of reentry, the administrative system also plays a significant role. Individuals may need to navigate various administrative processes, such as applying for identification documents, accessing public benefits, and finding housing. Understanding these processes is crucial to successfully reintegrating into society. In this section, we will provide an overview of the administrative processes individuals may encounter during reentry and explain their importance in the overall reentry journey.

Understanding administrative agencies and programs:

To navigate the administrative system effectively, individuals need to understand the roles and functions of various administrative agencies and programs. Agencies such as the Department of Motor Vehicles, Social Security Administration, and public housing authorities play a pivotal role in providing essential services and benefits to individuals going through reentry. In this section, we will explore the functions of these agencies and programs, equipping individuals with the knowledge they need to interact with them confidently.

Applying for benefits and services:

Applying for benefits and services can be a complex process, often requiring individuals to gather necessary documentation and meet eligibility requirements. This section will guide individuals through the application processes for different benefits and services, providing practical tips and resources to help them navigate the complexities. By understanding the application processes and requirements, individuals will be better prepared to access the support they need during reentry.

Building resilience:

Navigating the legal and administrative systems can be challenging, especially for individuals going through reentry. In this final section, we will offer strategies and resources for individuals to overcome these challenges and build resilience. Developing self-advocacy skills, seeking support from reentry programs or organizations, and engaging in self-care practices are just a few examples of the strategies that can help individuals navigate the legal and administrative systems successfully. By implementing these strategies and accessing available resources, individuals can maintain their emotional well-being and increase their chances of a successful reentry process.

By following the breakdown outlined in this subchapter, individuals will gain a comprehensive guide on understanding and successfully navigating the legal and administrative aspects of reentry. The knowledge and strategies provided will empower individuals to overcome challenges, advocate for themselves effectively, and ultimately reintegrate into society with confidence and resilience.

Dealing With Discrimination and Rejection

Introduction to Dealing with Discrimination and Rejection:

Throughout our lives, we inevitably encounter situations where we face discrimination and rejection. It's important to address and understand the potential impact these experiences can have on our emotional and psychological well-being. In this subchapter, our goal is to provide strategies for resilience in the face of discrimination and rejection.

Discrimination and rejection can have a profound effect on individuals, both emotionally and psychologically. The negative consequences are far-reaching, often resulting in decreased self-esteem, feelings of isolation, and even mental health issues. It's crucial that we explore the impact of these experiences so that we can better equip ourselves to navigate and overcome them.

Understanding the root causes of discrimination and rejection is key to addressing and combating them. Factors such as prejudice, stereotypes, and systemic biases contribute to these harmful experiences. By delving into the underlying causes, we gain a deeper understanding of the dynamics at play and can develop strategies to challenge and dismantle discriminatory practices.

Recognizing and addressing discrimination and rejection requires vigilance and assertiveness. It's essential that we become adept at identifying these experiences when they occur, and equally important to stand up for ourselves in the face of discrimination. By doing so, we not only protect our own well-being but also send a powerful message that discrimination will not be tolerated.

Coping mechanisms are invaluable tools for building resilience in the face of discrimination and rejection. Seeking support from loved ones, practicing self-care, and engaging in activities that promote self-confidence are just a few examples of effective coping strategies. By incorporating these techniques into our lives, we can bolster our ability to navigate and overcome the challenges we encounter.

Emotional resilience is a skill that can be developed, enabling us to better handle discrimination and rejection. Techniques such as mindfulness, reframing negative thoughts, and practicing self-compassion can all contribute to our emotional well-being. By intentionally cultivating emotional resilience, we equip ourselves with the tools necessary to face adversity head-on.

Building a support network is vital in navigating discrimination and rejection. Surrounding ourselves with individuals who provide emotional support, advice, and validation can make all the difference. A strong support network not only helps us weather the storm of discrimination but also empowers us to advocate for change and create a more inclusive society.

Promoting inclusion and equality is paramount in combating discrimination and rejection. It is incumbent upon us to advocate for change, challenge discriminatory practices, and strive to create a more inclusive society. By actively promoting inclusion and equality, we contribute to a more just and compassionate world.

Empowering others who have faced discrimination and rejection is a powerful way to create lasting change. Through mentorship, allyship, and advocacy, we can uplift those who have been marginalized and provide them with the tools and support they need to thrive. By harnessing our own experiences and resilience, we can make a meaningful impact in the lives of others.

Growth and resilience in the face of discrimination and rejection are ongoing processes. It is important to recognize that our journey towards empowerment and self-advocacy is ever-evolving. Let us continue to develop our resilience, empower ourselves and others, and strive towards a future where discrimination and rejection are no longer barriers to success and well-being.

Managing Emotional Triggers

In my journey of Restorative Reentry, one of the most crucial aspects I discovered was understanding and managing emotional triggers. These triggers play a significant role in our personal growth and well-being during the reentry process. They can have a profound impact on our emotions, behaviors, and overall mental health. In this chapter, we will explore what emotional triggers are, their varying nature, and how they can manifest in different ways.

Emotional triggers can be defined as specific events, situations, or stimuli that elicit an intense emotional response. These triggers are highly individualized and can vary from person to person. What may trigger a strong emotional response in one individual may not have the same effect on another. It is essential to recognize that emotional triggers are unique to each individual and can stem from a variety of sources.

Common types of emotional triggers include past traumas, unresolved relationship issues, and environmental factors. Past traumas can include experiences such as abuse, accidents, or significant losses. Relationship issues can stem from conflicts, betrayals, or unresolved emotional attachments. Environmental factors, such as certain places or situations, can also trigger emotional responses. For example, a person who experienced a traumatic event in a crowded place may feel anxious or overwhelmed in similar environments.

Emotional triggers can manifest in various ways, and it is crucial to recognize these signs and symptoms. They can include intense emotional reactions such as anger, fear, sadness, or even a sense of numbness. Physical manifestations can also occur, such as increased heart rate, sweating, trembling, or shallow breathing. Additionally, behavioral changes, such as avoidance, aggression, or withdrawal, may indicate the presence of an emotional trigger.

Recognizing these triggers is essential for self-awareness and personal growth. It allows us to understand ourselves better and gain insight into why certain situations or events have such a strong impact on us. There are several techniques that can aid in identifying emotional triggers, including journaling, therapy, and mindfulness practices. Journaling provides a safe space to reflect on our emotions and experiences, while therapy offers professional guidance and support. Mindfulness practices, such as meditation or body scanning, help us become more present and attuned to our emotions.

Understanding the root causes of our emotional triggers is vital for managing and coping with them effectively. Past experiences and conditioning often contribute to the development of these triggers. By exploring these underlying reasons, we can gain a deeper understanding of ourselves and our emotional responses. For example, someone who experienced a traumatic event in their childhood may develop triggers related to feelings of abandonment or betrayal. Identifying these root causes enables us to develop strategies to manage and cope with our triggers effectively.

Developing coping strategies is an essential part of managing emotional triggers. These strategies help us navigate and regulate our emotions when triggered. Various techniques can be employed, such as deep breathing exercises, grounding techniques, and positive self-talk. Deep breathing exercises, such as diaphragmatic breathing, can help calm our nervous system and reduce feelings of anxiety or panic. Grounding techniques, such as focusing on our senses or engaging in physical activities, can help bring us back to the present moment. Positive self-talk involves consciously replacing negative or irrational thoughts with more constructive and empowering ones. Moreover, prioritizing self-care and building a support network are crucial components of developing healthy coping mechanisms.

Cognitive restructuring plays a significant role in managing emotional triggers. This process involves challenging and reframing negative thoughts and beliefs. By identifying and replacing irrational or distorted thinking patterns, we can alter our emotional responses to triggers. For instance, if a person has a fear of public speaking and believes they will embarrass themselves, they can challenge this belief by gathering evidence of successful past experiences or seeking supportive feedback from others. Cognitive restructuring allows us to adopt more balanced and realistic perspectives, leading to healthier emotional responses.

Emotional regulation is another important aspect of managing emotional triggers. It involves developing skills to regulate and control our emotions effectively. Techniques such as practicing mindfulness, engaging in physical activity, and seeking professional help when needed can aid in emotional regulation. Mindfulness helps us become more aware of our emotions without judgment, allowing us to respond to triggers in a more intentional and balanced manner. Physical activity, such as exercise or yoga, can release endorphins and help alleviate stress or tension. Seeking professional help, such as therapy or counseling, can provide valuable guidance and support in developing healthy emotional regulation strategies.

To create a personalized trigger management plan, it is essential to identify specific triggers and implement coping strategies accordingly. This plan should be tailored to individual needs and preferences. Evaluating the effectiveness of the plan regularly allows for adjustments and improvements. Building resilience is a key outcome of managing emotional triggers. By effectively navigating and coping with triggers, we cultivate resilience, which contributes to improved emotional well-being and increased ability to face challenges. Cultivating resilience involves practicing self-compassion, setting realistic goals, and seeking support when needed.

Maintaining progress and continued growth is crucial in managing emotional triggers. Regular self-reflection and self-check-ins help us stay attuned to our emotional well-being and identify areas for improvement. Seeking feedback from trusted individuals or professionals can provide valuable insights and suggestions. Adapting coping strategies as needed ensures that our emotional well-being remains a priority. Finally, embracing the reentry journey as an opportunity for personal growth and transformation allows us to approach triggers with a sense of optimism and resilience.

Addressing Substance Abuse and Addiction

In this subchapter, I will be addressing the important topic of substance abuse and addiction during reentry. This is a relevant and significant issue for individuals who have been incarcerated and are transitioning back into society. Substance abuse and addiction are prevalent among those involved in the criminal justice system, and it is crucial to provide support and resources for individuals dealing with these issues as they reintegrate into the community.

Before diving into the specifics, it is essential to define key terms related to substance abuse and addiction. Terms such as substance use disorder, relapse, and recovery need to be clearly defined to avoid any misconceptions or stereotypes associated with them. Accurate terminology is vital in effectively addressing and supporting individuals with substance abuse issues during reentry.

The objectives of this subchapter are to provide resources and support for individuals dealing with substance abuse and addiction issues during reentry. We will cover a range of topics, including identifying risk factors, developing relapse prevention strategies, and accessing treatment options. It is important to note that this subchapter will focus on evidence-based practices and approaches, ensuring that we provide the most effective support to those in need.

To gather the necessary information, we have employed a methodology that involves reviewing current research, guidelines, and best practices in the field of substance abuse and addiction treatment. We also emphasize the importance of considering individual differences and tailoring interventions to meet the specific needs of individuals during reentry. A collaborative and multidisciplinary approach is necessary to provide effective substance abuse and addiction support.

Understanding substance abuse and addiction is essential to address the issue effectively. We will provide an overview of the neurobiological and behavioral factors involved in substance abuse and addiction. Additionally, we will discuss the impact of substance abuse and addiction on individuals' physical and mental health, as well as their social and occupational functioning. It is crucial to explore the cycle of addiction and the challenges individuals face in breaking free from substance abuse.

Identifying risk factors associated with substance abuse and addiction is crucial during reentry. We will identify common risk factors such as a history of trauma, co-occurring mental health disorders, and lack of social support. Recognizing and addressing these risk factors is essential in preventing relapse and promoting successful recovery.

Developing relapse prevention strategies is another critical aspect of addressing substance abuse and addiction during reentry. We will discuss the concept of relapse and the factors that can contribute to relapse in individuals with substance abuse issues. We will provide strategies for developing effective relapse prevention plans, including identifying triggers, building coping skills, and accessing ongoing support. It is important to involve support systems such as family members, friends, and treatment providers in the relapse prevention process.

Accessing treatment options is a significant challenge for individuals with substance abuse and addiction issues during reentry. We will explore various treatment options available, including outpatient counseling, residential treatment programs, and medication-assisted treatment. We will also address the barriers to accessing treatment, such as limited financial resources, lack of transportation, and stigma. Providing resources and information on overcoming these barriers will be essential in ensuring individuals can access appropriate treatment services.

Supporting long-term recovery is a crucial part of addressing substance abuse and addiction during reentry. Ongoing support and aftercare play a vital role in maintaining sobriety. We will provide information on support groups such as Alcoholics Anonymous and Narcotics Anonymous, as well as community-based resources that can assist individuals in maintaining their recovery. The role of probation and parole officers, as well as reentry programs, in providing continued support and monitoring during the reentry process will also be addressed.

Promoting community engagement and integration is key in supporting individuals with substance abuse and addiction issues during reentry. We will highlight strategies for promoting community acceptance, reducing stigma, and providing opportunities for individuals to rebuild their lives post-incarceration. Collaboration between community organizations, treatment providers, and criminal justice agencies is crucial in creating a supportive and inclusive environment for individuals in recovery.

In conclusion, addressing substance abuse and addiction during reentry is a vital aspect of supporting individuals as they transition back into society. By defining key terms, outlining objectives, exploring treatment options, and promoting community engagement, we can provide the necessary support and resources to individuals dealing with these issues. Through an evidence-based and collaborative approach, we can contribute to the successful reintegration of individuals with substance abuse and addiction issues.

Seeking Employment and Building a Career

In my book, Restorative Reentry, I want to emphasize the importance of job searching, resume building, and developing career pathways for individuals. These topics are crucial for individuals who are looking to reintegrate into society after being incarcerated. I believe that by providing guidance on these topics, I can help individuals find financial stability and personal fulfillment.

Job searching is a critical step in the reentry process. It not only helps individuals secure employment, but it also plays a significant role in their overall well-being. A steady job provides financial stability, allowing individuals to support themselves and their families. Additionally, being employed can greatly contribute to a sense of personal fulfillment and purpose.

To effectively navigate the job search process, I offer various tips and strategies. One of the most effective ways to find job opportunities is by utilizing online job boards. These platforms make it easy to search for openings in specific industries or locations. Networking is another crucial tool in the job search process. By connecting with professionals in their desired field, individuals can gain valuable insights and access to hidden job opportunities.

A well-crafted resume is essential for standing out in a competitive job market. I explain the different sections of a resume and provide guidance on tailoring it to specific job opportunities. I also offer tips for highlighting relevant skills and experiences, as well as formatting the resume for maximum impact.

Developing career pathways is crucial for long-term success. By having a clear career plan, individuals can set goals and work towards achieving them. I explore different ways individuals can develop their career pathways, such as through education, training, and professional development. I provide tips for setting career goals and creating a plan to reach them.

Building a professional network is another key aspect of career development. I explain the importance of networking and provide strategies for effectively building and maintaining professional relationships. Attending industry events, joining professional organizations, and utilizing social media platforms are all effective ways to expand one's professional network.

Job interviews can be nerve-wracking, but with proper preparation, individuals can increase their chances of success. I provide an overview of the job interview process and discuss different types of interviews. I also provide guidance on common interview questions and offer tips for presenting oneself professionally and confidently during interviews.

Negotiating job offers is an important skill to have. I emphasize the importance of advocating for oneself and securing favorable terms and conditions. I provide strategies for negotiating salary, benefits, and other job-related factors. It's important for individuals to conduct negotiations professionally and assertively to ensure they are getting the best possible offer.

Continuing education and professional development are vital for career growth. I highlight the importance of ongoing learning and provide an overview of different options for further education, such as certifications, online courses, and advanced degrees. Balancing work and education can be challenging, but I offer tips for maximizing the benefits of professional development opportunities.

Career transitions and advancement can be daunting, but they also present exciting opportunities. I discuss the challenges associated with career transitions, such as changing industries or moving up the corporate ladder. I also provide strategies for successfully navigating these transitions, including assessing skills and qualifications, setting goals, and seeking out opportunities for advancement.

Personal branding is crucial in today's job market. I explain the concept of personal branding and emphasize its importance in the job search and career development process. I discuss how individuals can identify and showcase their unique skills, experiences, and values. Building a strong personal brand through online presence, networking, and professional achievements is key to standing out from the competition.

By addressing these topics in detail and providing practical guidance, Restorative Reentry aims to empower individuals to successfully reintegrate into society, find meaningful employment, and build fulfilling careers.

Building a Positive Support System

Introduction to the Importance of a Positive Support System:

Having a positive support system is essential for personal growth and overall well-being. It encompasses the individuals who surround us and play a significant role in our lives. These individuals provide emotional support, encouragement, and guidance, helping us navigate through life's challenges. Conversely, negative influences can hinder our progress and drag us down. Recognizing the importance of a positive support system and actively seeking it out is crucial for creating a fulfilling and successful life.

Understanding the Impact of Surroundings on Mental Health:

Our mental health and overall well-being are greatly influenced by the people and environment around us. Research studies have consistently shown a correlation between positive support systems and improved mental health. When we surround ourselves with individuals who genuinely care for our well-being, we experience a sense of belonging and emotional security. These positive relationships contribute to building resilience and coping mechanisms, allowing us to navigate life's ups and downs with greater ease.

The Role of Positive Relationships in Building Resilience:

Positive relationships play a vital role in building resilience and fostering personal growth. Having individuals who provide emotional support and encouragement can make a significant difference in our ability to overcome challenges. These relationships serve as a source of strength during difficult times, enabling us to bounce back and grow from adversity. Surrounding ourselves with individuals who share similar values and goals can further enhance our journey towards personal growth and success.

Avoiding Negative Influences and Toxic Relationships:

In order to cultivate a positive support system, it is essential to identify and avoid negative influences and toxic relationships. These can include individuals who constantly bring us down, criticize our goals, or engage in harmful behaviors. Such influences can have a detrimental effect on our mental health and hinder our personal growth. By consciously distancing ourselves from these negative forces, we create space for positive relationships to flourish and support our journey towards self-improvement.

Strategies for Building a Positive Support System:

Building a positive support system requires intentional effort and the desire to surround ourselves with individuals who uplift us. One strategy is to seek out individuals who share similar values and goals. These like-minded individuals can provide support, understanding, and motivation as we pursue our aspirations. Additionally, actively participating in communities or groups centered around our interests can also help us connect with individuals who can contribute positively to our support system.

Developing Communication Skills for Positive Relationships:

Effective communication skills are crucial in maintaining positive relationships within our support system. By honing these skills, we can express ourselves clearly, resolve conflicts in a healthy manner, and strengthen our connections with others. Techniques such as active listening, empathy, and assertiveness can greatly improve our ability to communicate effectively and foster harmonious relationships.

The Role of Self-Reflection and Personal Growth:

Self-reflection plays a vital role in identifying and addressing negative influences in our lives. By taking the time to introspect and evaluate our relationships and surroundings, we can discern which individuals and environments uplift us and which ones hold us back. Personal growth and self-improvement are also integral to building a positive support system. When we continuously strive to better ourselves, we attract individuals who share our commitment to growth and surround ourselves with a supportive network.

Creating Boundaries and Setting Limits:

Setting boundaries in relationships and interactions is crucial for maintaining a positive support system. Boundaries help us establish healthy limits and protect our well-being. By clearly communicating our needs, values, and expectations, we can avoid negative influences and foster relationships built on respect and understanding. Boundaries act as a safeguard against toxic relationships, ensuring that our support system remains conducive to our personal growth and well-being.

Seeking Professional Support and Therapy:

In some cases, seeking professional support and therapy can be instrumental in building a positive support system. Therapists and counselors provide a safe space to explore our emotions, overcome past traumas, and develop strategies for personal growth. Different types of therapy, such as cognitive-behavioral therapy or group therapy, offer unique avenues for support and guidance. Utilizing these resources can augment our existing support system and provide us with the tools necessary to navigate through life's challenges.

Continuously Nurturing and Maintaining a Positive Support System:

Building a positive support system is not a one-time endeavor, but an ongoing process that requires continuous effort. It is important to actively contribute to our support system by reciprocating the support and encouragement we receive. Taking the time to celebrate the successes of our support network, offering assistance when needed, and expressing gratitude for their presence in our lives helps nurture and maintain a strong and lasting support system. By investing in our relationships and remaining mindful of their significance, we ensure that our support system remains a pillar of strength throughout our personal journey.

Key Takeaways

Introduction to Key Takeaways:

In Restorative Reentry, I dive deep into the process of reintegrating into society after a period of incarceration. Throughout the book, I emphasize the importance of key takeaways - those main points that summarize the core lessons and insights covered in each chapter. These takeaways serve as valuable tools for readers, enabling them to distill the most crucial information and apply it to their own lives. By highlighting the key takeaways in this introduction, I aim to provide a roadmap for readers to navigate through the chapters and extract the most valuable lessons for their own restorative reentry journey.

First Key Takeaway:

The first key takeaway in Restorative Reentry is the recognition that personal growth is a continuous process. I explore the idea that change doesn't happen overnight and that it requires consistent effort and self-reflection. By delving into the details of this key point, I emphasize the significance of embracing growth as a lifelong journey, rather than expecting immediate transformation. This takeaway is crucial as it sets the tone for the rest of the book and establishes the mindset necessary for successful reentry.

Second Key Takeaway:

Building on the first takeaway, the second key point in Restorative Reentry delves into the power of self-belief. I explain how cultivating a strong sense of self-worth and belief in one's own abilities can significantly impact the reentry process. Through real-life examples and research findings, I illustrate the profound effects that positive self-belief can have on overcoming challenges and rebuilding one's life. By providing concrete evidence and practical applications, this takeaway empowers readers to cultivate self-belief as a foundational pillar of their restorative journey.

Third Key Takeaway:

Moving forward, the third key takeaway explores the importance of establishing a strong support network during the reentry process. I delve into the research and studies that highlight the positive impact of social connections and mentorship on successful reintegration. By emphasizing the role of supportive relationships, I guide readers in identifying and nurturing connections that can provide the necessary guidance and encouragement on their path to restoration.

Fourth Key Takeaway:

The fourth key takeaway delves into the significance of setting realistic goals and taking deliberate actions towards achieving them. I provide practical strategies and insights on how to set meaningful goals, break them down into manageable steps, and maintain motivation throughout the journey. By offering specific examples and techniques, I equip readers with the tools needed to navigate the complexities of goal setting and implementation.

Fifth Key Takeaway:

In the fifth key takeaway, I address the potential challenges and obstacles that individuals may face during the reentry process. From societal stigma to personal setbacks, I explore the various roadblocks that can hinder progress. By acknowledging these challenges and offering strategies to overcome them, I empower readers to navigate these obstacles with resilience and perseverance.

Sixth Key Takeaway:

Building on the previous takeaway, the sixth key point delves into the insights and perspectives gained from the reentry experience. I encourage readers to embrace their journey as an opportunity for self-discovery and personal growth. By sharing my own experiences and those of others who have successfully reintegrated, I highlight the transformative power of embracing one's past and using it as a catalyst for positive change.

Seventh Key Takeaway:

The seventh key takeaway in Restorative Reentry explores the connections and overlaps between the previous key points. By examining how these takeaways intertwine, readers gain a holistic understanding of the restorative reentry process. This key point serves as a reminder of the interplay between personal growth, self-belief, support networks, goal setting, overcoming challenges, and gaining insights throughout the journey.

Eighth Key Takeaway:

In the eighth key takeaway, I delve into potential areas for further exploration and research within the realm of restorative reentry. I invite readers to engage with the material beyond the scope of the book, encouraging them to delve deeper into the topics covered and contribute to the growing body of knowledge surrounding restorative reentry.

Ninth Key Takeaway:

The ninth key takeaway offers a personal reflection on the restorative reentry journey. Drawing on my own experiences and insights, I share anecdotes and reflections that provide readers with a deeper understanding of the emotional and psychological aspects of the process. This takeaway adds a personal touch to the book, fostering empathy and connection with readers.

Tenth Key Takeaway:

In the final key takeaway, I synthesize the main points covered throughout the chapter, drawing key insights and conclusions. I offer readers a summary of the core lessons and encourage them to reflect on their own restorative reentry journeys. By providing a sense of closure and resolution, this takeaway serves as a launching pad for readers to apply the lessons learned to their own lives.

Throughout Restorative Reentry, these key takeaways serve as guideposts, enabling readers to navigate the complexities of the reentry process. By distilling the main points into these succinct and actionable takeaways, I aim to empower readers to embark on their restorative journeys with confidence and clarity. Restorative reentry is a transformative process, and by embracing these key takeaways, readers can maximize their potential for growth and success.

Resources for Further Learning

As someone who has faced my fair share of challenges, I understand the value of having additional resources to support and guide me through difficult times. Throughout my journey, I have come to appreciate the importance of resources in providing the necessary information and tools to overcome obstacles and thrive. In this chapter, we will explore a range of resources that can help readers facing specific challenges, offering support, guidance, and knowledge.

One of the most easily accessible and convenient resources available to readers today is the vast array of online platforms and websites. These digital resources provide a wealth of information and support, catering to a wide range of challenges. Whether it's forums dedicated to specific topics, online courses, or interactive tools, the online world offers a multitude of options. The beauty of these resources lies in their accessibility, as they can be accessed anytime, anywhere, allowing readers to take advantage of their convenience and flexibility.

Books and literature play a crucial role in providing in-depth knowledge and insights into specific challenges. Unlike online resources, books offer a deep dive into a particular subject, providing a comprehensive understanding that can be hard to find elsewhere. Whether it's memoirs, self-help books, or educational literature, these written resources offer a wealth of information that can guide readers on their journey to restorative reentry. Books not only educate and inform, but they also inspire and provide a sense of connection, making them invaluable resources for personal growth and development.

Educational organizations are another valuable resource for readers facing specific challenges. These organizations offer specialized programs, courses, and support tailored to address specific issues. Whether it's vocational training, skill development, or educational programs, these organizations provide readers with the necessary tools and resources to overcome their challenges and create a successful future. The expertise and guidance offered by educational organizations can be instrumental in helping readers navigate their way through difficult times and achieve their goals.

Support groups and communities play a vital role in providing resources for readers. These groups offer emotional support, shared experiences, and practical advice to those facing similar challenges. Being part of a supportive community can make a significant difference in one's journey to restorative reentry. By connecting with others who have faced similar obstacles, readers can gain valuable insights and guidance, while also finding comfort in knowing they are not alone.

Mental health services are of utmost importance in providing resources for readers. These services offer counseling, therapy, and resources for mental well-being, which are essential components of restorative reentry. Mental health professionals can provide the necessary support and guidance to help readers navigate their emotional and psychological challenges. By addressing mental health needs, readers can lay a solid foundation for their overall well-being, allowing them to tackle other challenges more effectively.

Government agencies and programs also offer a range of resources for readers facing specific challenges. These agencies provide assistance, funding, and support to individuals seeking to overcome obstacles and reintegrate into society. From employment programs to housing assistance, government resources can make a significant impact on the journey to restorative reentry. By accessing these programs, readers can receive the necessary support to address their specific challenges and achieve their goals.

Nonprofit organizations are another invaluable resource for readers. These organizations often have a specific mission and focus on providing targeted resources to individuals facing specific challenges. Whether it's financial assistance, mentorship programs, or advocacy services, nonprofit organizations offer a wide range of support to readers in need. The passion and dedication of these organizations make them an essential part of the restorative reentry process.

Specialized services cater to the unique challenges faced by readers. These services offer expertise, guidance, and resources tailored to address specific issues. Whether it's legal assistance, addiction recovery programs, or job placement services, specialized services provide readers with the tools and support they need to overcome their challenges. By tapping into these resources, readers can gain valuable insights and access the necessary resources to successfully navigate their journey to restorative reentry.

Community centers and libraries serve as invaluable sources of resources for readers. These institutions offer access to information, workshops, and community events that can support readers on their journey. Community centers provide a space for individuals to connect, learn, and grow together, while libraries offer a wealth of knowledge and literature that can guide readers on their path to restorative reentry. By utilizing the resources available in these community spaces, readers can gain valuable insights, connect with others, and access the support they need to thrive.

In conclusion, the importance of resources cannot be overstated when it comes to facing specific challenges. Whether it's online platforms, books and literature, educational organizations, support groups, mental health services, government agencies, nonprofit organizations, specialized services, or community centers and libraries, these resources offer support, guidance, and knowledge to readers on their journey to restorative reentry. By utilizing these resources, readers can empower themselves, overcome obstacles, and create a fulfilling and successful future.

Chapter 8: Restorative Reentry in Action

Personal Stories of Transformation

Introduction and Problem Statement

In this subchapter, I aim to share inspiring personal stories of individuals who have successfully reintegrated into society using restorative practices. The purpose of these stories is to provide hope and encouragement to individuals who are facing similar challenges. Reintegrating into society after a period of incarceration or other life challenges can be extremely difficult. The problem being addressed here is the lack of support and resources available to these individuals, which often leads to high rates of recidivism.

The Power of Personal Stories

Personal stories have a unique power to inspire and motivate others. They provide a glimpse into the lives of individuals who have overcome significant obstacles and achieved personal transformation. By sharing their stories, we can show others that change is possible and give them the hope and courage to pursue their own journey of reintegration.

These stories can also serve as a source of hope and encouragement for individuals who are facing similar challenges. When someone sees that another person has successfully reintegrated into society, it can help them believe that they too can overcome their own obstacles and create a better future for themselves.

Story 1: From Incarceration to Entrepreneurship

Let me introduce you to John, a former inmate who transformed his life from incarceration to successful entrepreneurship. After serving a lengthy prison sentence, John was determined to turn his life around. Through the support of restorative practices and a strong network of mentors, he was able to start his own business and become a thriving member of society.

John's journey was not easy. He faced numerous challenges along the way, from the stigma associated with his past to the difficulties of starting a business with limited resources. However, with the help of restorative practices such as counseling, job training programs, and support from his community, he was able to overcome these obstacles and create a better future for himself.

Story 2: Overcoming Addiction and Rebuilding Relationships

Next, let me share the story of Sarah, who battled addiction and rebuilt her relationships. Sarah's struggle with addiction had taken a toll on her life and strained her relationships with her loved ones. However, through restorative practices such as therapy, support groups, and the love and forgiveness of her family, she was able to overcome her addiction and rebuild the trust and connection with those who mattered most to her.

Sarah's journey towards recovery was not linear, and she faced many setbacks along the way. However, she never gave up and continued to seek help and support from her community. With the help of restorative interventions, she was able to transform her life and create a strong foundation for her future.

Story 3: Finding Purpose and Giving Back

Now, let me introduce you to Mark, who found purpose and gave back to society after experiencing a traumatic event. Mark's life was turned upside down after a tragic accident that left him questioning his purpose and meaning. Through restorative practices such as therapy, community involvement, and self-reflection, he was able to find a new sense of purpose and make a positive impact on the lives of others.

Mark's journey towards finding purpose was not easy, and he had to confront his own demons and fears along the way. However, with the support of his community and the restorative practices he engaged in, he was able to turn his life around and use his experiences to inspire and uplift others.

Story 4: From Gang Involvement to Community Leadership

Let me share the story of Alex, who transformed his life from gang involvement to community leadership. Alex grew up in a neighborhood plagued by gang violence and found himself getting involved in criminal activities at a young age. However, through restorative practices such as mentorship, education, and community outreach, he was able to break free from the cycle of violence and become a positive force in his community.

Alex's transformation was not without its challenges. He faced threats and resistance from his former associates, but he remained committed to his journey of change. With the help of restorative practices and the mentorship of individuals who believed in him, he was able to rise above his circumstances and become a leader in his community.

Story 5: Rebuilding a Life After Wrongful Conviction

Lastly, let me introduce you to Emily, who rebuilt her life after a wrongful conviction. Emily's life was shattered when she was wrongly convicted of a crime she did not commit. However, through restorative practices, legal support, and advocacy, she was able to prove her innocence and rebuild her life.

Emily's journey towards rebuilding her life was filled with obstacles and setbacks. She faced the challenges of rebuilding her reputation, finding employment, and rebuilding her relationships. However, with the support of restorative practices and the unwavering belief in her innocence, she was able to successfully reintegrate into society and create a new future for herself.

Common Themes and Lessons Learned

From these personal stories of transformation, several common themes and lessons emerge. One of the most significant lessons is the importance of restorative practices in facilitating personal transformation.

Whether it's counseling, support groups, mentorship, or community involvement, these practices provide the necessary tools and support for individuals to reintegrate successfully.

Another important lesson is the power of community support. In each of these stories, the individuals were able to transform their lives with the help of a strong support network. This support network provided the encouragement, resources, and accountability needed to navigate the challenges of reintegration.

Furthermore, personal resilience and determination are key factors in the journey of reintegration. These individuals faced significant obstacles and setbacks, but they never gave up. Their stories remind us that no matter how challenging the circumstances may be, with the right support and mindset, it is possible to overcome and create a better future.

Inspiration and Call to Action

In conclusion, the inspiring personal stories shared in this subchapter demonstrate the transformative power of restorative practices and the resilience of the human spirit. By reading these stories, we are reminded that change is possible, and that we can make a difference in the lives of others.

I encourage you, the reader, to take action. Whether it's supporting restorative practices, volunteering, or sharing your own personal story of transformation, you have the power to create change. Together, we can build a society that embraces and supports individuals in their journey of reintegration, and in doing so, we can create a more compassionate and inclusive world.

Restorative Organizations and Programs

Introduction to restorative reentry practices:

Restorative reentry is a revolutionary concept that has the power to transform the criminal justice system as we know it. It goes beyond traditional punitive measures and focuses on healing, rehabilitation, and rebuilding individuals and communities affected by crime. In this introduction, I aim to shed light on the importance of restorative reentry practices and the positive impact they can have on individuals and communities.

Restorative reentry is a philosophy rooted in the belief that every person has the capacity for change and growth. It recognizes that incarceration alone is not enough to address the root causes of crime and that a holistic approach is needed to support successful reintegration into society. By prioritizing accountability, empathy, and healing, restorative reentry practices aim to break the cycle of crime and create a safer, more just society.

The positive impact of restorative practices cannot be overstated. Studies have shown that when individuals are given the opportunity to take responsibility for their actions, make amends, and be supported in their journey of transformation, they are more likely to reintegrate successfully into society. This not only reduces recidivism rates but also promotes healing and reconciliation for all parties involved.

Overview of restorative organizations:

Several organizations have recognized the transformative potential of restorative reentry practices and have implemented them in their work. These organizations serve as beacons of hope, offering a new approach to the criminal justice system. Let me introduce you to some of these trailblazing organizations and the populations they serve.

First, we have Organization A, a nonprofit dedicated to providing comprehensive support to individuals transitioning from incarceration to community life. Their mission is to break the cycle of recidivism by empowering individuals with the skills, resources, and support they need to reintegrate successfully. Through a combination of mentorship, counseling, job training, and community engagement, Organization A equips their participants with the tools to rebuild their lives and become productive members of society.

Next, we have Organization B, a grassroots initiative that focuses on restorative justice practices for juvenile offenders. Their goal is to address the underlying causes of youth crime and promote accountability, empathy, and healing. Organization B employs unique approaches, such as circle sentencing and victim-offender mediation, to foster dialogue and understanding between offenders, victims, and the community. By encouraging active participation from all stakeholders, Organization B aims to create a sense of ownership and responsibility for the harm caused and facilitate the healing process.

Case study 1: Organization A:

Now, let's delve deeper into Organization A's restorative reentry program and explore the specific practices and strategies they employ to support successful reentry.

Organization A's program begins with an intensive needs assessment to identify the individual's strengths, challenges, and goals. This assessment serves as the foundation for creating a personalized reentry plan that addresses the unique needs of each participant. The plan includes a range of services, such as individual and group counseling, life skills workshops, educational support, and job placement assistance.

One of the key strengths of Organization A's program is their focus on mentorship. They pair each participant with a trained mentor who serves as a source of support, guidance, and accountability throughout their reentry journey. The mentor not only helps navigate the challenges of reintegrating into society but also acts as a positive role model, inspiring and motivating the participant to stay on track.

In addition to mentorship, Organization A recognizes the importance of community involvement in the reentry process. They actively engage community members through restorative justice circles, where participants, mentors, and community members come together to share experiences, build understanding, and foster a sense of belonging. This collective approach promotes social integration and reduces the stigma often associated with individuals who have been incarcerated.

The impact of Organization A's program has been nothing short of remarkable. Participants consistently report increased self-esteem, improved interpersonal skills, and a sense of purpose. Moreover, the recidivism rates among program graduates are significantly lower compared to those who did not participate. These success stories and testimonials speak volumes about the transformative power of restorative reentry practices.

In conclusion, restorative reentry practices offer a new paradigm for the criminal justice system, one that prioritizes healing, rehabilitation, and community engagement. By highlighting the impact and success stories of organizations like Organization A, we can begin to imagine a future where restorative reentry is the norm rather than the exception.

Mentorship and Peer Support

Introduction:

Mentorship and peer support play crucial roles in the restorative reentry process. In this chapter, I will define what mentorship and peer support entail in the context of reintegrating individuals into society after incarceration. We will explore the significance of these forms of support in helping individuals successfully navigate the challenges of reentry and create positive behavioral changes. Additionally, we will discuss how mentorship and peer support contribute to reducing recidivism rates, ultimately promoting a more sustainable and inclusive society.

Understanding the Role of Mentors:

Mentors have a vital role in the restorative reentry process. They are responsible for providing guidance, support, and advocacy to individuals who are reintegrating into society. These mentors possess specific qualifications that enable them to effectively assist individuals in their journey towards successful reentry. By sharing their own experiences and knowledge, mentors can empower individuals, helping them make informed decisions and navigate various challenges they may face.

Successful mentorship relationships have had a profound impact on the reentry process. For instance, mentors can help individuals develop important life skills, connect them with resources and opportunities, and serve as positive role models. Through these relationships, individuals gain confidence, hope, and a sense of direction, all of which are crucial in establishing a solid foundation for a successful reentry into society.

The Benefits of Peer Support:

Peer support plays a crucial role in the restorative reentry process by creating a sense of belonging and connection for individuals. It allows them to interact with others who have similar experiences and understand the unique challenges they face during reentry. Through shared experiences, individuals can find empathy, understanding, and a supportive community that promotes their well-being and personal growth.

Peer support groups provide a safe space for individuals to share their struggles, gain valuable insights from others, and develop essential life skills. These groups foster a supportive environment where individuals can explore different coping mechanisms, discuss common challenges, and celebrate milestones together. Ultimately, peer support networks empower individuals to develop resilience, self-confidence, and a sense of belonging, all of which contribute to a successful reentry process.

Identifying Potential Mentors and Peer Support Networks:

To maximize the benefits of mentorship and peer support, it is important for individuals to identify potential mentors within their communities. Finding mentors with similar backgrounds or experiences enhances relatability and understanding, ensuring effective guidance and support. Community organizations, support groups, and even social media platforms can serve as valuable resources for connecting with potential mentors and peer support networks.

Establishing Effective Mentorship Relationships:

Building strong and supportive mentorship relationships requires effort and intentionality from both parties involved. Individuals seeking mentors should set clear goals, establish boundaries, and maintain open lines of communication. These guidelines enable mentors to effectively guide individuals through the challenges of reentry and provide valuable feedback and support.

Creating a Supportive Peer Network:

Building a supportive peer network during the reentry process is essential. These networks provide individuals with the necessary encouragement, understanding, and accountability to navigate the complexities of reintegration. Strategies for connecting with peers include attending support group meetings, joining online communities, and participating in activities that foster camaraderie and mutual support.

Overcoming Challenges in Mentorship and Peer Support Relationships:

Challenges may arise in mentorship and peer support relationships, but they can be overcome with strategies such as conflict resolution, managing expectations, and maintaining trust. Ongoing support and guidance are crucial for both mentors and peers to ensure the sustainability of these relationships.

Measuring the Impact of Mentorship and Peer Support:

To advocate for increased support and resources for mentorship and peer support initiatives, it is important to evaluate their effectiveness. Various methods can be used to measure the impact, including tracking recidivism rates and conducting research to identify positive outcomes associated with mentorship and peer support. These data-driven approaches are essential for showcasing the value and impact of these programs.

Success Stories and Testimonials:

Personal stories and testimonials from individuals who have benefited from mentorship and peer support can inspire and motivate others. These stories highlight the transformative impact of mentorship and peer support on their lives, offering valuable lessons and insights into the restorative reentry process.

Conclusion and Call to Action:

In conclusion, mentorship and peer support are vital components of the restorative reentry process. By defining these forms of support and highlighting their importance, we have seen how they contribute to successful reintegration and reducing recidivism rates. I encourage readers to seek out mentorship opportunities and peer support networks, both as recipients of support and potential mentors themselves. Together, we can create a more inclusive and supportive society for individuals going through the reentry journey.

Reentry as Advocacy

Introduction to the concept of reentry as advocacy:

I have always been fascinated by the power of personal stories to inspire and motivate. There is something incredibly moving about hearing someone share their experiences of triumph and resilience in the face of adversity. This is especially true when it comes to individuals who have successfully reintegrated into society after incarceration. Their stories of overcoming the challenges of reentry and rebuilding their lives are not only inspiring, but they also serve as a powerful tool for advocating for restorative reentry.

When we talk about reentry as advocacy, we are referring to the idea that individuals who have gone through the process of reintegrating into society after incarceration can play a crucial role in advocating for others who are going through the same journey. Their lived experiences give them a unique perspective and credibility that can be incredibly impactful in inspiring others to believe in their own potential for change.

However, it is important to acknowledge the challenges that individuals face during the reentry process. The stigma surrounding a criminal record, coupled with a lack of support and limited opportunities, can make it incredibly difficult for individuals to successfully reintegrate into society. This is where advocates for restorative reentry come in. They understand the obstacles and work tirelessly to address them, creating a more supportive environment for those going through the reentry process.

The main conflict or problem that advocates aim to address is multifaceted. It could be the high rates of recidivism, where individuals find themselves trapped in a cycle of reoffending due to a lack of support and resources. It could also be the limited resources available for reentry programs, making it difficult for individuals to access the help they need to rebuild their lives. Lastly, it could be the negative public perception of individuals with criminal records, which perpetuates stereotypes and makes it harder for them to reintegrate into society.

Sharing personal success stories:

One of the most powerful tools in the advocate's arsenal is the ability to share personal success stories of individuals who have successfully reintegrated into society after incarceration. These stories serve as a beacon of hope for others who may be going through the reentry process, showing them that change is possible and that a brighter future awaits.

These success stories highlight the achievements of individuals who have not only overcome the challenges of reentry but have also gone on to thrive in their new lives. From finding stable employment to rebuilding relationships and overcoming addiction, these stories showcase the incredible resilience and determination of these individuals.

By sharing these success stories, advocates provide inspiration and motivation for others who may be struggling with the reentry process. They show that with the right support, guidance, and resources, it is possible to overcome the obstacles and build a new life after incarceration.

The role of advocates:

Advocates for restorative reentry play a vital role in supporting individuals who are reintegrating into society. They provide a range of support services, including guidance on navigating the reentry process, connecting individuals with resources and support networks, and advocating for policy changes and reforms to create a more supportive environment for reentry.

Advocates understand the unique challenges faced by individuals during the reentry process and work tirelessly to address them. They offer a listening ear, a shoulder to lean on, and a voice to speak up for those who may not have one. They provide guidance and support, helping individuals navigate the complex web of services and resources available to them. They also advocate for policy changes and reforms that will remove barriers and create a more inclusive and supportive environment for individuals with criminal records.

However, advocates themselves face their own set of challenges. Lack of funding is a common obstacle that many advocates encounter, making it difficult to provide the necessary support and resources to those who need it most. Resistance from policymakers can also hinder the progress of advocates, as they fight to change outdated policies and practices that perpetuate the cycle of reoffending. Additionally, effective advocacy often requires collaboration with various stakeholders, which can be challenging to navigate.

Despite these challenges, advocates for restorative reentry are resilient and determined. They understand that change takes time and effort, and they are willing to put in the work to create a more supportive and inclusive society for individuals who have been incarcerated.

Reaching a turning point:

In every advocacy journey, there comes a turning point that signifies progress and a step towards the ultimate goal. This turning point could be a successful campaign for reentry reform, where advocates successfully rally public support and mobilize policymakers to enact meaningful change. It could also be the establishment of a new program or initiative that fills a gap in reentry services, providing much-needed support to individuals transitioning back into society. Another turning point could be a significant policy change that removes barriers and creates a more inclusive environment for individuals with criminal records.

No matter the form it takes, this turning point is a cause for celebration and a testament to the power of advocacy. It represents the progress made in promoting restorative reentry and serves as a source of inspiration for advocates and individuals going through the reentry process alike.

Celebrating the impact and inspiring others:

The impact of advocating for restorative reentry cannot be overstated. Advocates have the power to change lives and transform communities. They have helped countless individuals reintegrate into society, providing them with the support and resources they need to rebuild their lives and achieve their goals.

By highlighting the positive outcomes of advocating for restorative reentry, we inspire others to join the cause. We show them the incredible impact that advocates have had and empower them to become advocates themselves. Through our collective efforts, we can create a ripple effect of change, spreading the message of restorative reentry and creating a society that supports and embraces individuals who have been incarcerated.

Sharing resources and tools:

To empower individuals to take action and make a difference, it is essential to provide them with the necessary resources and tools. There are various organizations dedicated to restorative reentry that individuals can join to connect with like-minded advocates and access additional support and resources. Training programs are also available to equip individuals with the knowledge and skills needed to effectively advocate for restorative reentry. Additionally, online platforms provide opportunities for engagement and networking, allowing individuals to connect with advocates and share their own stories and experiences.

By sharing these resources and tools, we give individuals the means to become advocates for restorative reentry. We provide them with the knowledge, support, and connections they need to make a real impact and contribute to the movement.

Closing thoughts:

In conclusion, reentry as advocacy is a powerful tool for creating change and transforming lives. By sharing personal success stories, advocating for policy changes, and providing support and resources, advocates play a crucial role in helping individuals successfully reintegrate into society after incarceration. The transformative power of reentry as advocacy lies in its ability to inspire and motivate others, ultimately working towards a society that supports and embraces individuals who have been incarcerated. Together, we can make a difference and create a brighter future for all.

Sustaining Restorative Practices

Restorative practices are not just for the reentry phase; they are essential for maintaining a balanced and fulfilling life. Beyond the challenges and barriers that individuals may face in sustaining these practices, it is crucial to understand the role of community support. Engaging with supportive communities can make a significant difference in maintaining restorative practices.

Building personal accountability is another crucial aspect. It involves taking responsibility for our actions and actively participating in the process of restoration. Strategies for building and maintaining personal accountability include setting clear goals, tracking progress, and holding oneself accountable to ensure continuous growth and development.

Cultivating empathy and compassion is equally important in sustaining restorative practices. Empathy and compassion allow us to connect with others on a deeper level and understand their experiences. Techniques such as active listening, perspective-taking, and practicing kindness towards oneself and others can help individuals strengthen their capacity for empathy and compassion.

Mindfulness and self-reflection play a fundamental role in sustaining restorative practices. By developing mindfulness and self-reflection as ongoing practices, individuals can become more aware of their thoughts, emotions, and behaviors. This self-awareness enables them to make conscious choices and respond to challenging situations with greater clarity and compassion.

Conflict resolution skills are vital for maintaining restorative practices. By developing effective communication and negotiation skills, individuals can navigate conflicts and disagreements in a constructive and restorative manner. Strategies such as active listening, seeking win-win solutions, and practicing non-violent communication can contribute to the resolution of conflicts in a way that promotes healing and understanding.

Addressing power dynamics is another critical aspect of sustaining restorative practices. Power imbalances can hinder the progress of restorative processes. Individuals must navigate and address these imbalances within the context of restorative practices to ensure equitable and just outcomes. By actively engaging in dialogue, promoting inclusivity, and challenging oppressive systems, individuals can work towards dismantling power structures that perpetuate injustice.

Advocating for restorative justice policies is an essential step in sustaining restorative practices. Restorative justice policies provide a framework for addressing harm and promoting healing within communities. By advocating for these policies, individuals can contribute to creating a more just and compassionate society.

Continued education and training are vital for individuals seeking to sustain restorative practices. It is essential to stay updated with the latest research, techniques, and best practices in the field. Resources and opportunities for further education and training, such as workshops, courses, and conferences, can help individuals enhance their knowledge and skills in restorative practices.

Creating a personal action plan is crucial for sustaining restorative practices. By developing a plan that aligns with their specific needs and goals, individuals can stay committed and focused on their journey towards restoration. This action plan should include specific steps, timelines, and milestones to track progress and hold oneself accountable.

In conclusion, sustaining restorative practices beyond the reentry phase requires dedication, support, and a comprehensive approach. By understanding the importance of community support, personal accountability, empathy and compassion, mindfulness and self-reflection, conflict resolution skills, addressing power dynamics, advocating for restorative justice policies, continuing education and training, and creating a personal action plan, individuals can navigate the challenges and embrace the transformative power of restorative practices.

Key Takeaways

Introduction to Key Takeaways:

In this subchapter, I want to emphasize the importance of the key takeaways that can be derived from the main points covered in this chapter. By summarizing these main points, we can gain a deeper understanding of the concepts and ideas discussed throughout the book. Through concise recaps and the inclusion of key details and information, we can ensure that these takeaways are both valuable and actionable.

Summary of Main Point 1:

One of the main points explored in this chapter is the significance of building a support network during the reentry process. It is crucial to surround yourself with individuals who can provide guidance, encouragement, and resources as you navigate the challenges of reintegration. By having a strong support system, you increase your chances of success and decrease the likelihood of relapse. Key details related to this main point include the importance of seeking out positive influences and actively participating in support groups or mentorship programs.

Summary of Main Point 2:

The second main point discussed in this chapter revolves around the need for personal growth and self-improvement during reentry. It is essential to focus on developing new skills, acquiring education or vocational training, and pursuing opportunities for personal growth. By investing in yourself, you not only enhance your chances of securing stable employment but also boost your self-confidence and overall well-being. Important concepts associated with this main point include the idea of continuous learning and the value of setting goals and working towards them.

Summary of Main Point 3:

Another key point explored in this chapter is the significance of addressing and managing past trauma and emotional wounds. Restorative reentry involves confronting and healing from the psychological scars that may have contributed to criminal behavior. By seeking therapy, participating in trauma-focused programs, and practicing self-care, individuals can better understand and address the underlying causes of their actions. Key elements related to this main point include the importance of forgiveness, self-reflection, and developing healthy coping mechanisms.

Summary of Main Point 4:

The fourth main point discussed in this chapter centers around the importance of building positive relationships and repairing damaged ones. Restorative reentry involves repairing the harm caused by past actions and rebuilding trust with loved ones and the community. By actively seeking reconciliation and demonstrating genuine remorse, individuals can mend broken relationships and foster a sense of belonging. Significant information and concepts linked to this main point include the idea of restorative justice, the role of empathy in repairing relationships, and the importance of accountability.

Summary of Main Point 5:

The fifth main point covered in this chapter highlights the significance of developing a strong sense of purpose and meaning in life. Restorative reentry involves discovering one's passions, interests, and values and aligning them with meaningful work or community engagement. By finding a sense of purpose, individuals can experience fulfillment, motivation, and a sense of contribution to society. Essential details and ideas related to this main point include the exploration of different passions, the importance of finding meaning beyond material success, and the benefits of engaging in volunteer work.

Summary of Main Point 6:

The sixth main point addressed in this chapter emphasizes the need for ongoing personal and professional development. Restorative reentry involves continuously improving oneself, acquiring new skills, and staying informed about current trends and opportunities. By investing in lifelong learning and adapting to the ever-changing world, individuals can remain relevant, competitive, and resilient. Notable information and concepts associated with this main point include the idea of embracing change, seeking out learning opportunities, and staying open-minded.

Summary of Main Point 7:

The seventh main point discussed in this chapter centers around the importance of self-advocacy and empowerment. Restorative reentry involves taking control of one's own life and actively pursuing opportunities for growth and success. By advocating for oneself, individuals can overcome barriers, assert their rights, and create positive change in their lives and communities. Key elements and ideas connected to this main point include the importance of self-belief, assertiveness training, and understanding one's rights and responsibilities.

Summary of Main Point 8:

The eighth main point covered in this chapter highlights the significance of financial literacy and stability during the reentry process. Restorative reentry involves developing financial skills, managing money effectively, and securing stable employment or entrepreneurial ventures. By becoming financially independent, individuals can reduce their vulnerability to recidivism and gain a sense of control over their lives. Important details and concepts linked to this main point include the value of budgeting, saving, and investing, as well as the importance of financial education and access to resources.

Summary of Main Point 9:

The ninth main point addressed in this chapter emphasizes the need for individuals to define success on their own terms. Restorative reentry involves rejecting society's narrow definitions of success and creating a personalized vision of fulfillment and accomplishment. By setting goals that align with one's values and aspirations, individuals can create a meaningful and purpose-driven life. Significant information and ideas related to this main point include the importance of self-reflection, goal-setting, and celebrating personal milestones.

Throughout this chapter, we have explored these main points in depth, providing insights, strategies, and resources for individuals seeking to reintegrate into society. By understanding and implementing these key takeaways, individuals can embark on a journey of restorative reentry, reclaiming their lives and building a brighter future.

Resources for Further Learning

Introduction and Setup:

Restorative reentry is a complex journey, fraught with challenges and uncertainties. As someone who has personally experienced the struggles of reentry, I understand the importance of having access to resources that can provide guidance and inspiration along the way. In this subchapter, "Resources for Further Learning," I aim to do just that – to offer a curated collection of resources that delve into restorative reentry success stories. By exploring these resources, readers can gain valuable insights, learn from others' experiences, and find the support they need to navigate their own reentry journey successfully.

Highlighting the Need for Further Learning:

Restorative reentry is not a straightforward process. It requires individuals to navigate a complex web of legal challenges, social stigmas, and personal obstacles. It is in this complexity that the need for further learning becomes evident. By expanding our knowledge and understanding, we can equip ourselves with the tools necessary to overcome these challenges. Whether it's learning about legal rights, building social connections, or developing personal resilience, further learning can provide individuals with the skills and knowledge they need to thrive in their reentry journey. Moreover, by studying success stories, individuals can find inspiration and guidance, discovering that they are not alone in their struggles and that a better future is possible.

Exploring Restorative Reentry Success Stories:

One of the most powerful ways to learn and gain insights is by exploring success stories of individuals who have gone through the process of restorative reentry. These stories serve as powerful learning tools, offering practical advice, emotional support, and a sense of hope. In this subchapter, I will delve into various types of success stories, including personal accounts, case studies, and documentaries. Each of these mediums offers a unique perspective and allows readers to engage with different aspects of restorative reentry. By exploring these diverse narratives, readers can gain a comprehensive understanding of the challenges and triumphs of reentry.

Books on Restorative Reentry Success Stories:

For those who prefer to dive deep into the subject matter, books are an invaluable resource. In this subchapter, I have curated a list of books that focus on restorative reentry success stories. Each book offers a unique perspective and explores different themes and lessons learned. From personal memoirs to academic studies, these books provide in-depth insights into the complexities of restorative reentry. By delving into these pages, readers can gain a deeper understanding of the challenges they may face and find inspiration in the stories of those who have successfully reintegrated into society.

Websites on Restorative Reentry Success Stories:

The internet is a treasure trove of information, and when it comes to restorative reentry, there are numerous websites that offer valuable resources. In this subchapter, I will introduce readers to a list of websites that provide resources on restorative reentry success stories. These websites offer a variety of content, including articles, videos, interviews, and forums. They provide up-to-date information, diverse perspectives, and a platform for individuals to connect and share their experiences. By exploring these websites, readers can access a wealth of information and engage with a supportive community dedicated to restorative reentry.

Documentaries on Restorative Reentry Success Stories:

Visual storytelling has a unique power to convey the triumphs and challenges of restorative reentry. In this subchapter, I will highlight a selection of documentaries that focus on restorative reentry success stories. Each documentary takes a different approach to storytelling, offering viewers an intimate and immersive experience. By watching these documentaries, readers can gain a deeper understanding of the emotional journey individuals go through during reentry and witness firsthand the transformative power of restorative justice.

Restorative Reentry Podcasts:

Podcasts have become increasingly popular in recent years, offering an intimate and personal exploration of various topics. In this subchapter, I will introduce readers to a collection of podcasts that delve into restorative reentry success stories. The podcast format allows listeners to hear firsthand accounts, conversations, and expert insights, providing a unique perspective on the challenges and triumphs of reentry. By tuning in to these podcasts, readers can gain valuable insights, practical advice, and a sense of connection to a larger community of individuals navigating restorative reentry.

Blogs and Personal Accounts:

There is immense value in hearing from individuals who have personally experienced restorative reentry. In this subchapter, I will introduce readers to blogs and personal accounts that provide firsthand narratives and reflections. These accounts offer relatable experiences, practical advice, and a sense of community. By reading these blogs and personal accounts, readers can find comfort in knowing that others have faced similar challenges and successfully reintegrated into society. These narratives can serve as a source of inspiration and guidance, reminding readers that they too can overcome the obstacles they may encounter on their reentry journey.

Online Communities and Forums:

The journey of restorative reentry can often feel isolating, but it doesn't have to be. In this subchapter, I will introduce readers to online communities and forums dedicated to restorative reentry. These platforms provide a space for individuals to connect, share their experiences, and offer support. They facilitate discussions on various aspects of reentry, ranging from legal challenges to mental health support. By engaging with these communities and forums, readers can find a sense of belonging and discover a network of individuals who understand the unique challenges they face.

Curating and Evaluating Resources:

The abundance of resources on restorative reentry can be overwhelming. In this subchapter, I will discuss the importance of curating resources and provide criteria for evaluating the quality and relevance of these resources. It is crucial to ensure that readers can trust and benefit from the recommendations provided. By curating resources, we can save readers time and effort in searching for reliable information and direct them towards resources that are most likely to meet their needs. This careful curation ensures that readers can make the most of their further learning journey and find the support they require to succeed in their restorative reentry process.

Conclusion:

In the journey of restorative reentry, the importance of further learning cannot be overstated. By exploring success stories through books, websites, documentaries, podcasts, blogs, and personal accounts, individuals can gain insights, find inspiration, and connect with a supportive community. By curating and evaluating these resources, we can provide readers with a roadmap to navigate the complexities of restorative reentry successfully. It is my hope that through these resources, readers will find the guidance and support they need to transform their reentry journey into a story of resilience, growth, and success.

Chapter 9: Conclusion

Reflecting on the Journey

Reflecting on my reentry journey has been a transformative experience. As I navigate the challenges of reintegrating into society after a period of incarceration, I have come to understand the power of self-reflection in acknowledging my progress. In this journey, I have faced numerous obstacles, both emotional and psychological, but through it all, I have recognized my personal growth and celebrated my achievements and milestones.

The reentry process is riddled with challenges that test one's resilience and determination. From finding employment and stable housing to rebuilding relationships and overcoming stigma, each step presents its own set of difficulties. The emotional and psychological impact of reentry cannot be overstated. It is a rollercoaster of emotions, as individuals grapple with feelings of shame, guilt, and uncertainty about their future. But it is through self-reflection that we can begin to understand the magnitude of these challenges and how far we have come.

Taking the time to reflect on our personal growth since embarking on our reentry journey is a crucial step in our progress. It allows us to acknowledge the positive changes we have made and recognize the strength and resilience we possess. By celebrating our progress, we build confidence and motivation to continue moving forward. It is important to remember that progress is not always linear, and setbacks are inevitable. But by reflecting on how we have overcome these obstacles, we gain valuable insight into our own strength and perseverance.

Identifying and celebrating achievements and milestones is a powerful tool for personal growth. By acknowledging the progress, we have made, we affirm our ability to overcome challenges and make positive changes in our lives. It is through this recognition that we find the motivation to keep pushing forward, even in the face of adversity. Recognizing our achievements also helps us build a sense of self-worth and confidence, which are essential for navigating the reentry journey.

Overcoming setbacks and challenges is an integral part of the reentry journey. Whether it is facing rejection in the job market or struggling to rebuild relationships, setbacks can feel disheartening. However, by reflecting on how we have overcome these obstacles, we gain a deeper understanding of our resilience and adaptability. We learn valuable lessons along the way and develop strategies for navigating future challenges.

Gaining perspective is essential in our reentry journey. It allows us to step back and see the bigger picture, understanding the progress we have made and the distance we have traveled. By viewing our journey from a broader perspective, we can appreciate the growth we have experienced and find inspiration to keep moving forward. Perspective reminds us that our reentry journey is part of a larger narrative, and that every step we take is a step towards a better future.

Building resilience is a key component of the reentry journey. It is the ability to bounce back from setbacks and keep moving forward. By reflecting on how our resilience has grown throughout the process, we gain a deeper understanding of our own strength and capacity for growth. Resilience is not something we are born with; it is something we cultivate through facing adversity and learning from our experiences.

Finding gratitude is a powerful practice that can transform our mindset and overall well-being. By expressing gratitude for the lessons learned and growth experienced during reentry, we shift our focus from the challenges to the opportunities for growth. Gratitude allows us to find joy in the journey, even during the most difficult times. It reminds us of our own resilience and the power we have to create positive change in our lives.

Setting future goals is crucial for continuing our progress on the reentry journey. By reflecting on our aspirations and dreams for the future, we create a roadmap for success. Goals provide us with direction and purpose, helping us to stay focused and motivated. They give us something to strive for and celebrate as we continue to grow and evolve.

In conclusion, reflecting on our reentry journey is a transformative process that allows us to acknowledge our progress, celebrate our achievements, and overcome setbacks. By gaining perspective, building resilience, and finding gratitude, we can continue to grow and thrive on our reentry journey. Setting future goals gives us direction and purpose, propelling us forward towards a brighter future. So let us reflect, celebrate, and continue to progress on our reentry journey, knowing that our growth and potential are limitless.

Continuing the Restorative Path

In this section, I want to talk about the importance of continuing on the restorative path, even after reentry. This chapter is all about offering guidance on how to embrace restorative practices in all aspects of life beyond the reentry process. I believe that sustaining these practices is not only crucial for personal growth but also for community development.

It's important to acknowledge that there are challenges individuals may face when trying to continue their restorative journey. One of these challenges is the impact of external factors such as social stigma, lack of support, and systemic barriers. These obstacles can make it difficult to maintain the restorative practices that have been learned during reentry.

Building a support network is crucial in overcoming these challenges. It's important to surround yourself with like-minded individuals who are also committed to restorative practices. This can be done by joining support groups, attending community events, or participating in online forums. By finding others who share your goals and values, you can create a strong support system that will help you stay on track.

Self-reflection and ongoing personal growth are also essential in sustaining restorative practices. It's important to engage in regular self-assessment, journaling, or even seeking therapy to address personal challenges and triggers. By continuously working on ourselves, we can ensure that we are able to maintain our commitment to restorative practices.

Accountability is another crucial aspect of sustaining restorative practices. Establishing accountability measures such as finding an accountability partner, setting goals, or joining a restorative justice circle can help keep us on track. Having someone to hold us accountable and support us in our journey can make a significant difference in our ability to continue embracing restorative practices.

Restorative practices can also be extended to our relationships beyond reentry. By applying these practices, we can resolve conflicts, build trust, and promote healthy communication. This can have a positive impact on our personal relationships and contribute to our overall well-being.

Incorporating restorative practices in the workplace can also be beneficial. By implementing restorative circles, conflict resolution processes, and fostering open communication, we can create a work environment that promotes healing and growth.

Restorative parenting techniques can also have a positive impact on family dynamics. By creating a nurturing and inclusive family environment that encourages open dialogue, empathy, and accountability, we can build stronger and healthier relationships with our loved ones.

Extending restorative practices beyond personal relationships and into the broader community is also important. Getting involved in community initiatives, volunteering with restorative organizations, or advocating for restorative justice policies can contribute to creating a more just and compassionate society.

Lastly, it's important to continue learning and growing in restorative practices. Pursuing further education, attending workshops or conferences, or participating in restorative justice training programs can enhance our understanding and application of these practices.

By embracing restorative practices in all aspects of our lives, we can continue on the path of healing and growth, not only for ourselves but for our communities as well. It is through these practices that we can create a more compassionate and restorative world.

Final Words of Encouragement

I believe in the power of encouragement. It has the ability to uplift and empower individuals on their ongoing journey of transformation. Encouragement plays a vital role in personal growth and development, as it has the potential to positively impact individuals by providing them with the motivation and affirmation they need. The simple act of offering positive words and affirmations can make a world of difference in someone's life.

Acknowledging and celebrating personal growth and accomplishments is essential. By recognizing progress and milestones, individuals are able to boost their motivation and self-esteem. It is important to take the time to acknowledge one's own growth and achievements, no matter how small they may seem. These acknowledgements serve as reminders of how far one has come and can be incredibly transformative.

Setting realistic goals and expectations is crucial for continued transformation. While it is important to dream big, setting unrealistic expectations can be detrimental to motivation and self-confidence. It is essential to set attainable goals that are within reach. By doing so, individuals can experience a sense of accomplishment and stay motivated on their journey of transformation. Managing expectations is also important, as it allows individuals to maintain a healthy perspective and avoid unnecessary disappointment.

Embracing the journey of transformation is a mindset that we must adopt. This process is not linear and is filled with ups and downs, setbacks, and challenges. It is important to view these obstacles as opportunities for growth rather than reasons to give up. By sharing personal stories or examples, I hope to inspire readers to persevere and stay committed to their personal growth, no matter what challenges they may face.

A growth mindset is crucial for ongoing transformation. By adopting a growth mindset, individuals are able to embrace the idea that they can continue to learn, develop, and evolve. This mindset increases resilience and motivation, as individuals believe in their ability to overcome obstacles and achieve their goals. I will provide practical tips and strategies for cultivating a growth mindset, so readers can apply them to their own journey of transformation.

Self-doubt and fear are common obstacles that can hinder personal transformation. It is important to address these challenges and provide strategies for overcoming self-doubt and managing fear. By sharing stories or examples of individuals who have successfully overcome self-doubt and fear on their transformational journey, I hope to inspire readers to push through their own limitations.

Building a supportive community is crucial for sustained transformation. Having a network of like-minded individuals who can provide encouragement and support is invaluable. Whether it is joining support groups or seeking out accountability partners and mentors, building a supportive community can make a significant difference in one's journey of personal growth.

Cultivating self-compassion and self-love is essential throughout the transformational journey. Practicing self-acceptance, forgiveness, and nurturing oneself are vital components of personal growth. I will provide practical exercises and techniques for readers to cultivate self-compassion and self-love, allowing them to develop a strong foundation for their ongoing transformation.

Staying resilient in the face of challenges is crucial. Obstacles and setbacks are inevitable, but it is resilience and adaptability that allow individuals to overcome these challenges and stay motivated. I will share strategies and techniques for developing resilience, such as reframing challenges and practicing gratitude. By developing these skills, readers will be equipped to navigate any obstacles that come their way.

Continued growth is a lifelong journey. Even after achieving initial goals, it is important to keep pushing forward and embracing new challenges and opportunities. Personal development is a continuous process, and there is always room for growth.